MONKS OF MT. TABOR

WISDOM
DISTILLED FROM THE DAILY

·S· BENEDICT·

Wisdom
DISTILLED FROM
THE DAILY

Living the Rule of St. Benedict Today

JOAN D. CHITTISTER, O.S.B.

1817

Harper & Row, Publishers, San Francisco

New York, Grand Rapids, Philadelphia, St. Louis
London, Singapore, Sydney, Tokyo, Toronto

This book is dedicated to my community—the
Benedictine Sisters of Mount Saint Benedict
Monastery, Erie, Pennsylvania—whose lives
make this work possible and these words true.
With love and pride.

References to the Rule are from Fry, Timothy, O.S.B., et al. *RB80*. Collegeville, MN: Liturgical Press, 1981 and Schauble, Marilyn, O.S.B., and Wojciak, Barbara, O.S.B., eds. *A Reader's Version of the Rule of Saint Benedict in Inclusive Language*. Erie, PA: Benet Press, 1989.

The stories and references of the Desert Monastics are taken from *The Sayings of the Desert Fathers* translated by Benedicta Ward, S.L.G. Kalamazoo, MI: Cistercian Publications, Inc., 1975.

Basic scriptural reference is *The New American Bible*. Nashville: Thomas Nelson, Inc., 1971.

Source of reference on Page xxx is Butler, Cuthbert, O.S.B. *Benedictine Monachism*. London: Longmans, Green and Co., 1919.

Library of Congress Cataloging-in-Publication Data

Chittister, Joan.
 Wisdom distilled from the daily : living the Rule of St. Benedict
today / Joan Chittister.
  p. cm.
  ISBN 0-06-061351-3
  1. Benedict, Saint, Abbot of Monte Cassino. Regula.
 2. Benedictines—Rules. 3. Benedictines—Spiritual life.
 4. Spiritual life—Catholic authors. I. Title.
 BX3004.A2 1990
 255'.106—dc20   89-45557
                     CIP

90 91 92 93 94 RRD 10 9 8 7 6 5 4 3 2 1

Table of Contents

Acknowledgments   vii

1. The Rule: A Book of Wisdom   1
2. Listening: The Key to Spiritual Growth   14
3. Prayer and *Lectio*: The Center and Centrifuge of Life   27
4. Community: The Basis of Human Relationships   39
5. Humility: The Lost Virtue   51
6. Monastic Mindfulness: A Blend of Harmony, Wholeness, Balance   67
7. Work: Participation in Creation   80
8. Holy Leisure: The Key to a Good Life   95
9. Giftedness: Making Music Together   108
10. Hospitality: The Unboundaried Heart   121
11. Obedience: Holy Responsibility   133
12. Stability: Revelation of the Many Faces of God   147
13. Monastic Practices: The Way of Conversion   160
14. Peace: Sign of the Disarmed Heart   181

15.   The Monastic Vision: Gift for a Needy   194
      World

Appendix   208

Glossary   213

Acknowledgments

It would be very strange, I think, if a book about community life could ever be done alone. This one, at least, certainly was not.

I am especially indebted to those people who read the manuscript from multiple perspectives and provided both fine suggestions and encouraging responses. Particular among them are Lawreace Antoun, S.S.J., Marlene Bertke, O.S.B., Robert Bilheimer, Mary Collins, O.S.B., Patrick Henry, Mary Lou Kownacki, O.S.B., Johnette Putnam, O.S.B., Barbara Thomas, SCN, Marlene and Jerry Trambley, Barbara and Virgil Roseborough, and Anne Vinca.

Manuscript preparation takes precision and commitment. Without Stephanie Campbell, O.S.B., Mary Grace Hanes, O.S.B., and Mary Ann Luke, O.S.B., believe me, this one would not have seen the light of day.

Thanks to Marcie Bircher, O.S.B., the artwork in the text links the present interpretation of Benedictine spirituality with its tradition in very classic form.

No one I know is able to write unless someone else smooths the way, maintains the daily obligations that get suspended during long days of intense concentration, and prods the work through its long, dark periods. In this case all of that and more was done, both for me and the community, by Maureen Tobin, O.S.B., subprioress of the monastery.

The inspiration for the work really came from Jan Johnson, my editor at Harper & Row, whose own insights and interest first envisioned this work.

Finally, I acknowledge with gratitude the contributions of the community that has formed me and made this life and these reflections possible.

1

The Rule:
A Book of Wisdom

Are you hastening toward your heavenly home? Then with
Christ's help, keep this little rule that we have written for beginners. After that, you can set out for the loftier summits of the
teaching and virtues we mentioned above, and under God's pro-
tection you will reach them. Amen.

RB 73:8–9

The ancients tell a story of the spiritual life
that may best explain this book:

A young monastic came upon an elder one day sitting
among a group of praying, working, meditating people.

"I have the capacity to walk on water," the young disciple
said. "So, let's you and I go onto that small lake over there and
sit down and carry on a spiritual discussion.

But the Teacher answered, "If what you are trying to do is
to get away from all of these people, why do you not come
with me and fly into the air and drift along in the quiet, open
sky and talk there."

And the young seeker replied, "I can't do that because the
power you mention is not one that I possess."

And the Teacher explained, "Just so. Your power of remaining still on top of the water is one that is possessed by fish.
And my capacity of floating through the air can be done by any

fly. These abilities have nothing to do with real truth and, in fact, may simply become the basis of arrogance and competition, not spirituality. If we're going to talk about spiritual things, we should really be talking here."

Just about every person I have ever met who was serious about spiritual things thinks the point of the story is true: daily life is the stuff of which high sanctity can be made. But just about nobody I have ever met, however, really thinks it is easily possible. Spirituality, we have all learned somehow, is something I have to leave where I am in order to find it. I get it in small doses, in special places and under rarefied conditions. I hope I get enough at one time in life to carry me through all the other times. The idea that sanctity is as much a part of the married life or the single life as it is of the religious life or the clerical life is an idea dearly loved but seldom deeply believed.

In our own times, too, just as at the time of the story, fads crowd into the spiritual life. We are told that novenas are the answer one year and retreats another and meditation centers a third. True believers tell us that the cult of their choice is the only answer to the struggles of life. The occultists promise salvation in the stars or from ancient oriental lore. The therapeutic community offers marathon encounters or anger-release workshops to cleanse the soul. Over and over again, cures and cults and psychological exercises are regularly tried and regularly discarded while people look for something that will make them feel good, steady their perspective, and bring meaning and direction to their lives. But, as the ancient story demonstrates, if we are not spiritual where we are and as we are, we are not spiritual at all. We are simply consumers of the latest in spiritual gadgetry that numbs our confusions but never fills our spirits or frees our hearts.

After years of monastic life I have discovered that unlike spiritual fads, which come and go with the teachers or cultures that spawned them, the Rule of Benedict looks at the world through interior eyes and lasts. Here, regardless of who we are or what we are, life and purpose meet.

The Rule of Benedict has been a guide to the spiritual life for common people since the sixth century. Anything that has lasted that long and had that kind of impact in a throwaway society is certainly worthy of consideration. This book looks at these questions. "How do we account for a way of life that has lasted for over fifteen hundred years, and what, if anything, does it have to say to the spiritual life in our world today?"

Benedictine spirituality offers exactly what our times are lacking. Benedictine spirituality seeks to fill up the emptiness and heal the brokenness in which most of us live in ways that are sensible, humane, whole, and accessible to an overworked, overstimulated, overscheduled human race.

The Rule of Benedict called the class-centered Roman world to community and calls us to the same on a globe that is fragmented. The Rule called for hospitality in times of barbarian invasions and calls us to care in a world of neighborhood strangers. It called for equality in a society full of classes and castes and calls us to equality in a world that proclaims everyone equal but judges everyone differently. Benedict, who challenged the patriarchal society of Rome to humility, challenges our own world, too, whose heroes are Rambo and James Bond, military powers and sports stars, the macho and the violent.

Benedictine spirituality calls for depth in a world given over almost entirely to the superficial and the tinny. It offers a set of attitudes to a world that has been seduced by gimmicks and quick fixes. Benedictine spirituality offers insight and wisdom where pieties have lost meaning and asceticisms have lost favor.

Most of all, Benedictine spirituality is good news for hard times. It teaches people to see the world as good, their needs as legitimate, and human support as necessary. Benedictine spirituality doesn't call for either great works or great denial. It simply calls for connectedness. It shows us how to connect with God, with others, and with our inmost selves.

All in all, the Rule of Benedict is designed for ordinary people who live ordinary lives. It was not written for priests or mystics or hermits or ascetics; it was written by a layman for laymen. It was written to provide a model of spiritual development for the average person who intends to live life beyond the superficial or the uncaring. It is written for people with deeply spiritual sensibilities and deeply serious concerns who have no intention of setting out to escape their worlds but only to infuse their moral lights with the vision of the Divine.

The Rule of Benedict is wisdom distilled from the daily. This book is simply an account of how I, having lived this Rule in a monastic community for over thirty years, have come to understand the implications of a Benedictine spirituality for our own times.

Spirituality is more than churchgoing. It is possible to go to church and never develop a spirituality at all. Spirituality is the way in which we express a living faith in a real world. Spirituality is the sum total of the attitudes and actions that define our life of faith.

For the apostle Paul, spirituality meant living "in Christ" and seeing the gifts of the Spirit as gifts meant to "build up the Body of Christ" here and now. But understandings of what constituted the perfect Christian life changed from period to period across the ages. It was equated, variously, with martyrdom and withdrawal and evangelization and self-denial. By the period in the church closest to our own, for instance, spirituality had come to mean being obedient to "duly constituted superiors" and able to arouse a great deal of emotional response in private prayer. Spirituality, or "life according to the Spirit," was measured for many by the number of masses attended or the number of rosaries said or the number of commands accepted with docility or the number and kinds of things that were "given up" in order to lead a higher or more "perfect" life. As a result of those criteria, only nuns, monks, and priests were credited with really being able to live the spiritual life. This understanding persisted until Vatican II with its recognition of the universal call to holiness and the authenticity of the lay vocation in the Church.

We are beginning again, as people did in earlier times, to see the spiritual life through a wider angle lens. The spirituality we develop affects the way we image God, the way we pray, the types of asceticism we practice, the place we give to ministry and community in our definition of "the spiritual life." It is spirituality that draws us beyond ourselves to find significance and meaning in life. It is our spirituality that defines our life values: self-abnegation or self-development; community or solitude; contemplation or evangelization; personal transformation or social justice; hierarchy or equality. The spirituality we develop, in other words, is the filter through which we view our worlds and the limits within which we operate.

The spirituality that emerges from the Rule of Benedict is a spirituality charged with living the ordinary life extraordinarily well. Here transforming life rather than transcending it is what counts. That's why the Rule of Benedict is meant for hard-working, busy people whose family lives and bills and civic duties and hard work consume them in this world today as well as for those who have dedicated themselves to living a publicly professed religious life.

The question is, What are the spiritual values enshrined now for nearly fifteen hundred years in the Rule of Benedict and what do they have to say, if anything, to our own age and our own attempts to live calmly in the middle of chaos, productively in an arena of waste, lovingly in a maelstrom of individualism, and gently in a world full of violence? What do they have to say to us who seek answers to the great questions of life while our work overwhelms us and our debts expand, while our families vie for our attention and our friends minimize our concerns, while our politicians tell us that life is getting better when we know that, for many at least, much in life is actually getting worse.

Like the seekers in the story, most of us cannot rush to the sea for distance or fly away to other places for escape. Most of us must simply live where we are, in the midst of the crowds and the complex questions. Most of us have no other access to God and the good life except *now*, except *here*. The problem becomes discovering how to make here and now, right and holy for us. The here and now is all we have, any of us, out of which to make life worthwhile and God present and holiness a normal, rather than an unnatural, way of life.

For people like us, Benedictine spirituality is home. Benedictine spirituality deals totally in the here and now. Benedictine spirituality is made out of the raw material of the average daily life. It assumes no great asceticisms and promises no great spiritual feats. It asks for no great physical denials and gives no great mystical guarantees. It describes no specific life work and depends on no great organizational plan. The Rule of Benedict simply takes the dust and clay of every day and turns it into beauty.

The Rule of Benedict is not a set of spiritual exercises and not a set of proscriptions and not a set of devotions and not a set of disciplines. The Rule of Benedict, in fact, is not a rule at all, in the modern sense of that word.

Where "rule" is interpreted to mean controls or laws or demands, the Rule of Benedict does not qualify for that category. On the contrary. The Rule of Benedict is simply a plan of life, a set of principles that is clearly meant to be nearer to the original meaning of the Latin word *regula*, or guide, than to the concept *lex*, or law. Law is what we have come to expect from religion; direction is what we need.

Regula, the word now translated to mean "rule," in the ancient sense meant "guidepost" or "railing," something to hang on to in the dark, something that leads in a given direction, something that points out the road, something that gives us support as we climb. The Rule of Benedict, in other words, is more wisdom than law. The Rule of Benedict is not a list of directives. The Rule of Benedict is a way of life.

And that's the key to understanding the Rule. It isn't one.

That's why it can be just as important to lay people

as it is to monastics. "Listen ... whoever you are," Benedict says in the Prologue to the Rule. *Whoever* you are.

The Rule of Benedict is simply a piece of Wisdom Literature designed to deal with the great questions of life in ways that make them understandable and present and clear and achievable.

But coming to realize that in both a church and a world that want either all law or no law at all is not easy. Formula and license are so much simpler than steady, steady attention to the quality of life we are creating as well as seeking. It is very difficult when we're young, in other words, to realize that to get where we want to go in life we must often do things we would not choose to do. To rise early in the morning to pray and read is very foreign thinking to the corporate climber who is sure that what really needs to be done is to store up sleep and conserve strength for the difficult day ahead. To the monastic mentality, though, nothing more sensible can possibly occur. Without the praying and the reading, the monastic believes, who will ever understand what the climbing is meant to reach or the achieving is all about? To halt work for prayer in the middle of a chaotic day seems, to many a young monastic whose work or study is magnetizing and good, to be sheer unreality. But years later it becomes clear that the daily process of stopping to remember what life is really all about at its *giddiest* peaks may have been the only unvarnished reality of that whole period of life.

It is attention and awareness, in other words, that the Rule of Benedict brings to spirituality. Indeed, the very reason the rule of Benedict is not a rule in the strictest sense of the word is precisely because immersion in life is exactly the point of Benedictine monasticism. Benedictinism is not a prescription frozen in time; it is time brought under the scrutiny of gospel values. The Benedictine does not set out to avoid life; the Benedictine sets out to live the ordinary life extraordinarily well. As a result, the real monastic is alive to the world.

Monasteries hardly seem like places from which to analyze the world. To go to the monastery, popular mythology has it, is to leave the world, not to get even more deeply involved with it. But it may be only from a distance that we see best. It may be those who do not have money who best know that money is not essential to the good life. It may be those who each have only a bed and books and one closet full of clothes in one small room to call their own who can clearly realize what clutter can do to a life. It may be those who vow obedience to another who can sense what self-centeredness can do to corrode the heart. It may be only those who stand alone in life who can really know what community is all about. It may be those who are powerless by choice who can best demonstrate the power that comes from not having power. It may be those who have decided against amassing personal property who can realize that bankruptcy and welfare and sufficiency are not the worst things that can happen to a person in life. It may be those who are unmarried by choice who can most sensitively hear the abandoned and the widowed and the lonely. It may only be those who have no corporate or ecclesial ladder to climb who can best speak to equality. Indeed, the monastery gives a privileged perspective from which to speak to the world.

Once you realize that the text of the Rule of Benedict is only one element of the monastic life it becomes evident that its other three dimensions are very clearly intended to keep a person grounded in the real world. The gospel of Christ, the interpretations of community leaders, and the lived experience and insight of each particular community itself, are as much the Rule as the Rule itself. It is those dimensions that give the Rule life and breadth, depth and scope, antiquity and relevance, local character and universal possibility. Those four elements—the Scriptures, the text of the Rule, wise leaders, and the insight, life experiences, and circumstances of the community or family in which we live—are what make the Rule a living rule and not a dead text of past practices, not a historical document, not the pastime of eccentric antiquarians.

The Rule of Benedict lives and breathes from age to age. The Rule of Benedict examines and adapts from one century and culture to another. The Rule of Benedict guides people to an attitude of mind but does not smother them with sets of particular prescriptions. The Rule of Benedict is written for our lives and our circumstances as much as it was for any time past. It grows with the times and goes with the times and gives us a grasp, a railing, a guide that will not allow us to be ground down to spiritual nothingness and personal torpor by our own times.

The monastic looks for holiness in the here and now, unburdened by strange diets or esoteric devotions or damaging denials of self. The real monastic walks through life with a barefooted soul, alert, aware, grateful, and only partially at home.

So, what does it mean to follow the Rule of Benedict, to think with a monastic mind-set, to live life more as gift than as struggle?

First, a Benedictine spirituality is a commitment more

to principles than to practices. The Benedictine does not so much follow an horarium, or rigid daily schedule, as arrange a balance of life activities. The Benedictine does not so much follow a set of behaviors as develop an attitude of place in the universe that guides every conversation and every common act. Benedictine spirituality is more about living life well than about keeping the law perfectly.

Second, Benedictine spirituality is simply a guide to the Gospels, not an end in itself. Benedict calls his rule "a little rule for beginners" (RB 73:8) in the spiritual life, not a handbook for the elite, or the literati, or the accomplished. Housewives and househusbands, maestros and career women, monastics and lay people, "all you who seek the Heavenly home" (RB 73:8), the Rule urges, not to spiritual gymnastics but to the contemplative awareness that the gospel and the gospel alone is fit criteria for any human action.

Third, the Rule shows clearly that the living of the gospel life is not an individual enterprise of private whim and flights of personal fancy but a conscious gathering of the wisdom of others who can encourage us and help us scrutinize our own choices for their value and their valor.

Finally, Benedictine spirituality rests squarely on the notion that we are not the only measure of our own spiritual needs but that the entire human community and cosmic universe have claim on the merit of our daily actions.

In a world in which the planet has become the neighborhood and our personal lives are made up of unending streams of people, the Rule of Benedict with its accent on the spiritual qualities of life lived in common may never have been more relevant. I have begun to see under the covers of this age-old monastic rule a semblance of sanity to the insanity of the world around me.

When I first entered monastic life, I was given a copy of the Rule. It made no sense to me. I wanted directions. I wanted a formula. I wanted holiness on the installment plan: buy now, pay later. It took me years to understand that if I paid now, I would get what I was looking for only if and when I had become what I sought. It took me years to realize that the Rule distilled years of experience, a kind of memoir of what Benedict believed spiritual life was all about and a record of what apparently had been the most effective ways of achieving it for that time. But it was not a blueprint at all.

In Chapter 72 of the Rule, Benedict warns us about "wicked zeal," the fanaticism and absolutism that make religion an instrument of oppression against ourselves and others. In Chapter 73, he promises, "If you fulfill this least rule . . . then you shall attain at last to the greater heights of knowledge and virtue." I began to see this life would take constancy and patience and balance. We were into growth here, not into practices. This life would be about the sanctification of the normal, not about spiritual gymnastics. We were about a way of life, not about living life a certain way.

As a result, I now find myself going to the Rule of Benedict when I wonder what the Christian response to ecological problems should be. I go to the Rule to find my way through the thickets of human relationships. I rely on the values and principles of the Rule to tell me how to deal with life's vagaries. I look to the Rule to explain my depression and my frustration and my spiritual ennui. I depend on the Rule to help me get my mind off me. I see the Rule as a set of values that transcend time but have special meaning for my own days.

I have written this book to share these years of reflections with people who I have found are just as serious about the questions and just as concerned about the way as I am. In the face of continuing confusions, shall we go back and be the old Church? Would that solve our dilemmas? Or is any church our answer in this day and age when churches themselves struggle with the nuclear questions, the woman's question, the life-style questions, the pastoral questions, the family questions, the personal questions of alienation and unrest? What is spirituality in the midst of all of that: a rosary a day, meatless meals, a regular retreat, involvement on parish committees, public activism? The questions crescendo. The answers, I think, reside in things that neither come nor go with the years and the times. The answers lie in bringing wisdom, not recipes, to bear.

These pages are my reflections on the wisdom that emerges in an ancient text about our very old, very new concerns. To live the Benedictine Rule, it is not a set of mechanics we need; it is a change of heart and a turn of mind.

Once upon a time, an ancient monastic tale says, the Elder said to the businessperson:

"As the fish perishes on dry land, so you perish when you get entangled in the world. The fish must return to the water and you must return to the Spirit."

And the businessperson was aghast. "Are you saying that I must give up my business and go into a monastery?" the person asked.

And the Elder said, "Definitely not. I am telling you to hold on to your business and go into your heart."

This book is intended to help average people see today's world through the filter of the Rule of Benedict and the yearnings of our own hearts.

2

Listening: The Key to Spiritual Growth

Listen carefully, my child, to the master's instructions, and attend to them with the ear of your heart. This is advice from a parent who loves you; welcome it, and faithfully put it into practice.

Let us open our eyes to the light that comes from God, and our ears to the voice from heaven that every day calls out this charge: "If you hear God's voice today, do not harden your hearts" (Ps. 94[95]:8). And again: "You that have ears to hear, listen to what the Spirit says to the churches" (Rev. 2:7). And what does the Spirit say? "Come and listen to me and I will teach you the fear of God" (Ps. 33 [34]:12). "Run while you have the light of life, that the darkness of death may not overtake you" (John 12:35).

RB PROLOGUE: 9–13

The bells that ring over every Benedictine monastery are an archaic way to get a group's attention to the order of the day, and, if that were their only purpose, there are surely better ways to do it. Buzzers and clocks and public-address announcements and blinking lights, for a few, would certainly do a better, more efficient job. But Benedictine bell towers are about more than the schedule of the day. Benedictine bell towers are designed to call the attention of the world to the fragility of the axis on which it turns. Benedictine bell towers require us to listen even when we would not hear.

Years ago, when I was a young monastic, we were taught that when the clock chimed the hour we were to stop whatever we were doing and say the hour prayer. It was an old formula, long since dropped, and it is not remembered in its entirety by anyone in the community anymore. But we all know what it was meant to do. It was meant to make those of us who lived on missions away from the monastery where our bells did not ring, conscious over and over again of the frailty of life and the demanding presence of God in the minute by minute circumstances of our lives.

"Listen," the Rule says.

"Listen," the bell says.

"Listen," monastic spirituality says.

And listening is what Benedictine spirituality is all about in a culture that watches but very seldom hears.

Benedictine spirituality is about listening to four realities: the Gospels, the Rule, one another, and the world around us. Most of us listen easily to one or two of these realities, but only with difficulty do we listen to all four. We read the Scriptures faithfully but fail to apply them. We listen to the needs of the poor but forget the reading of the gospel entirely. We go to spiritual directors regularly but ignore or overlook the insights of the people with whom we live. We prefer to hear ourselves than to listen to wiser hearts for fear they might call us beyond ourselves. Benedictine spirituality requires the medley.

One of the monastics of the desert taught the truth this way:

A young seeker asked the Teacher, "I have received a command to do a good work, but there is danger of temptation in the place where I would have to go to do it. Because of the command, I wish to do it, but I am afraid of the danger."

And the old Teacher said, "If it were my problem, I would fulfill the commandment and that way I would be sure to overcome the temptation."

The spiritual life, in other words, is not achieved by denying one part of life for the sake of another. The spiritual life is achieved only by listening to all of life and learning to respond to each of its dimensions wholly and with integrity.

The bells that call monastics to prayer ring outside the chapel as well as inside the monastery. They summon us from where we are to what we need to think about if the work we go on doing is to be pure and promising and prophetic. They lead us to where we can bring the Word of God to bear upon our own.

The Rule of Benedict refers to Scripture as the voice of Christ (RB Prologue:19), a divine medicine (RB 28:3), and a weapon against the devil (RB Prologue:28). We listen to Scripture, in other words, to shield us from lesser motives. Scripture, prayed intently, calls us back on dull days to the overriding purpose of life. When nothing seems to have a purpose, Scripture puts us into direct contact with the Christ who seems, really, so far away from the office and the kitchen and the street corner. Scripture heals us of our own narrowness or smallness or struggles with faith in an age that says the purpose of life is to get ahead of our friends and be number one and make money and get prestige and put our faith in instruments of terror called a nuclear shield. Through all of this, the Scriptures bring us to watch the great figures of the gospel working through their own struggles of faith in times that were, for them, equally as perilous as ours. Benedictine spirituality depends on our listening to the Scriptures and finding a simple, practical way to live that good news outside the chapel, where we were when the bells first called us and where we will go again once we remind ourselves why we were doing what we were doing at the sound of the bell in the first place.

Prayer in Benedictine spirituality is not an interruption of our busy lives nor is it a higher act. Prayer is the filter through which we learn, if we listen hard enough, to see our world aright and anew and without which we live life with souls that are deaf and dumb and blind.

But prayer can be an easy substitute for real spirituality. It would be impossible to have spirituality without prayer, of course, but it is certainly possible to pray without having a spirituality at all. There are business people of our generation, for instance, who go to prayer breakfasts regularly and then raise interest rates on Third World debts and increase mortgage rates on housing loans and refuse aid to farmers but easily advance money to munitions companies. There are people who go to prayer groups and never give a cent to the poor. And there are monastics who go to chapel and forget that the function of reading the gospel is to become a gospel person, not an ecclesiastical hothouse plant.

The fact is that the way Satan gets to the holy person may be through sanctity. "The wicked zeal," Benedict calls it, "which leads to separation from God" (RB 72:1). Even sanctity, we're being warned, can become a barrier to growth. Unless we can hear the needs of the other as well as the words of our favorite prayers, the prayer itself may be worth nothing more than hypnotic hollowness. It may make us feel like good people, but it will hardly make us better people.

We prayed a great deal when I was a young nun. We prayed seven times a day for over three hours in all. In another language. On a rigid schedule. But no one ever came into our dining room. No poor slept in our houses. No children cried in our chapels. No refugees came to our doors. No one even thought to look to us for clothing or shelter or support or conviction about anything. We lived in one world. People lived in another. And we all prayed.

Today, too, people go faithfully from church to neighborhood week after week and, then, between times give themselves entirely to making money and being nationalistic and having fun. In the meantime, Lazarus again waits hungry for the Christians of this time to notice his deprivation and stoop down to listen to him as the Lazarus of the gospel story waited in vain for help from the wealthy and pious Dives.

The Rule of Benedict clearly emphasizes the need to listen to the people with whom we live as well. Benedict, who began religious life as a hermit—the norm for the time—soon left the cave to live in community and listen to the demands and insights both of the shepherds in the hills around him and of the monastics who gathered around him. No one was excluded from the role of heavenly messenger: "Receive the guest as Christ" (RB 53:1), he said. "Let the Abbot ask everyone beginning with the youngest" (RB 3:4). In monastic spirituality, life together—despite Sartre's cynical suggestion that "Hell is other people"—is an opportunity for the presence of God to manifest itself, not an obstacle to it.

Not to listen, then, is not to grow. But more than that,

to be unable to listen is to be unable to give as well. It is easy to know what is good for someone else. It is difficult to listen and let them define themselves. Benedict puts the entire Rule in one sentence when, as his last will and testament of community, he says at the end of it, "Anticipate one another with honor, most patiently enduring one another's infirmities, whether of body or character; vie in paying obedience to one another, tender love chastely, fear God in love; love one another" (RB 72:4–10). It takes a lot of listening to hear the needs of those around us before they even speak them. But there is no good human community without it. Listening and love are clearly of a piece.

Benedictine listening is about more than attending to the Scriptures, praying, and being sensitive to the needs of those around us, though. Benedictine listening is about seeking out wise direction as well. It is one thing to try to hear what is in front of us. It is another to willingly expose our ideas to the critical voice of a wiser heart.

Seeking wise direction—as the monastic does by living in the community and trusting its elders, its wise, its holy ones, its simple ones—is central to personal growth. Wives do that for husbands; husbands do that for wives; parents do that for children; counselors do that for clients; employers do that for employees. We must all learn to listen to the truths of those around us. We are poor shadows of listening hearts if we think that listening has something to do with simply taking orders. No, listening has something to do with being willing to change ourselves and change our world. Listening is a religious discipline of the first order that depends on respect and leads to conversion.

It's a point we so often forget. Wrapping ourselves up in the womb of religious ritual is no substitute for genuine spirituality. Spirituality is not an exercise in blind obedience, it is a commitment to divine reflection. The bells ring out around a monastery to alert people around us that we are listening to the Word of God, to put the world on notice that we may be different now, to warn the universe that we are trying to hear more clearly the whisper of God in the gentle breezes of life.

The Word of God has never been for its own sake. The Word of God has always impelled. The Word of God sent Abraham and Moses and Mary and Mary Magdalene into totally new levels of commitment and consciousness. And the Word of God demanded no less intense degrees of commitment and consciousness when it came through Mordecai to Esther, through Samuel to Eli, through Elizabeth to Zachary. When we start listening to the Word of God, to others around us, to those with wise hearts and tried souls, life changes from the dry and the independent to the compassionate and the meaningful. When we start listening to the Word of God, people have a right to expect something new of us.

But the Benedictine spirituality of listening puts us in dangerous territory. If we really listened to the Gospels, we would question a life-style that endlessly consumes and hoards and is blind to the homeless and unconcerned about the unprepared. How is it possible to listen to the Scripture about the rich young man, or the blind leper, or the grieving widow, and not know that in this century all the miracles for today's poor and outcast and crippled depend on us? If we really listened to the people with whom we lived, could we bear to see children neglected or partners ignored or neighbors rejected? If we really took the thoughts of our hearts and the hopes of our lives to those wiser and holier than we for examination, how could we tolerate situations that could have and should have been ended before they began to eat away at our best selves?

The Rule teaches us to listen to the circumstances of our own lives. We have to begin to face what our own life patterns might be saying to us. When we are afraid, what message lurks under the fear: a horror of failure, a rejection of weakness, panic at the thought of public embarrassment, a sense of valuelessness that comes with loss of approval? When we find ourselves in the same struggles over and over again, what does that pattern say: That I always begin a thing with great enthusiasm only to abandon it before it is finished? That I am always reluctant to change, no matter how good the changes might be for me? That I keep imposing unsatisfactory relationships with people from my past on every new person I meet? That down deep I have never given myself to anything except myself? Not to my friends. Not to my work. Not to my vocation.

Until I learn to listen—to the Scriptures, to those around me, to my own underlying life messages, to the wisdom of those who have already maneuvered successfully around the dangers of a life that is unmotivated and unmeaningful—I will really have nothing whatever to say about life myself. To live without listening is not to live at all; it is simply to drift in my own backwater.

Listening is, indeed, a fundamental value of Benedictine spirituality. More than that, Benedictine listening is life lived in stereo. The simple fact is that everybody lives listening to something. But few live a life attuned on every level. Benedictine spirituality doesn't allow for selective perception; it insists on breadth, on a full range of hearing, on total alert. We have to learn to hear on every level at once if we are really to become whole. The problem is that most of us are deaf in at least one ear.

We have to learn to listen to Scripture. And we have to learn to listen to life around us.

Scripture, the Rule insists, must be read daily. How can we hear the voice of God if we are not familiar with it? How can we recognize the ways of God if we have never seen them? How can we discover the will of God in our own lives if we have never traced its clear but jagged paths in the lives of the chosen weak before us? Indeed, Scripture is basic to a Benedictine life, but it is just as important to hear God's voice in the world around us. And there, perhaps, is the real test of the listening heart. It does not take much to hear in our own language. What takes sanctity is to be able to hear in the tongue of the other.

- People in positions of authority know they aren't being heard if the people they are trying to direct turn every conversation into an adolescent struggle with the ghosts of their parents.
- The poor know that the rich cannot hear them because success has deafened them. The rich cannot hear the voices of those unable to get the cleaning or the ditch-digging or the dishwashing jobs that people of past generations took for granted in their climb to the top.
- Women know that men don't hear or take seriously their concerns for children or education or independence or equal wages and full human options.

- The isolated elderly know that power talks and they no longer have it.
- Families soon discover whose voice carries weight, whose will is sacred in the house, who does not listen and who will not respond.
- The lonely know that no one is listening to their need for love and laughter.
- The Church knows that worship has become more a duty than a dialogue for some, more therapeutic than prophetic for others.

Our entire generation has gone deaf. Scripture and wisdom and relationships and personal experience are all being ignored. We are, consequently, a generation of four wars and of the most massive arms buildup in the history of the world—in a period called peacetime. We are a generation of great poverty in the midst of great wealth, of great loneliness in the center of great communities; of serious personal breakdowns and community deterioration in the face of unparalleled social growth; of great spiritual ennui in the middle of our great claims of being a God-fearing country.

Into the midst of all this indistinguishable cacophony of life, the bell tower of every Benedictine monastery rings "listen." Listen with the heart of Christ. Listen with the lover's ear. Listen for the voice of God. Listen in your own heart for the sound of truth, the kind that comes when a piece of quality crystal is struck by a metal rod.

The problem is, perhaps, that most of us don't even know what listening involves. But the Rule tells us clearly.

First, Benedict requires that everything must be done with counsel. Benedictine spirituality has no room for arrogance elevated to the level of inspiration. To cultivate a monastic mentality, we must seek counsel, take advice, listen to the opinion of others on subjects dear to us. Reflection becomes integral to the process of growth and basic to our style of acting. Impulsiveness becomes suspect even when the impulsive decision turns out to be right. Why? Because truth is a mosaic of the face of God. Because the voice of God comes often from where we would least expect it, like a burning bush or a stranger or a dream or a messenger from afar or a prophet of the court. And we must be listening for it.

Second, Benedict teaches, life is a learning process. Western culture and its emphasis on academic degrees, however, has almost smothered this truth. We have made the words "graduation" and "education" almost synonymous. We measure achievement in academic credits. We discount experience, depth, and failure. We believe in action and results and products and profit and youth, so we come to regard the elderly as essentially useless.

But, in the end, all of that kind of achievement is nothing but a spiritual wasteland if along the way we have not attached ourselves to the discovery of truth, the cultivation of beauty, and the recognition of the real learnings of life.

Benedictine spirituality is, then, the spirituality of the open heart. A willingness to be touched. A sense of otherness. There is no room here for isolated splendor or self-sufficiency. Here all of life becomes a teacher and we its students. Here certification alone does not count as qualification. The listener can always learn and turn and begin again. The open can always be filled. The real disciple can always be surprised by God. "Listen with the ear of the heart" (RB Prologue:1), the Rule instructs.

But once I become my own message there is nothing else to hear. No way to grow. No chance to change. Nothing but echoes of my own voice.

At one point in the monastic life, I was sure that knowing the Rule and practicing its practices was the secret of the holy life. Now I know that knowing the document will never suffice for listening to the voice of God, wherever it may be found. No longer do I hope that someday, somehow, I will have accumulated enough listening so that there will be no further questions about pious practices that can easily be learned. Now I have only a burning commitment to those qualities of the spiritual life that must be learned if I am to grow.

Once upon a time, an ancient story tells, there was a seeker who had heard of the Fruit of Heaven and who coveted it.

The seeker asked a teacher, "How can I find this fruit, so that I may attain to immediate knowledge?"

"You would be best advised to study with me," the Teacher said. "If you will not do that, you will have to travel resolutely and at times restlessly throughout the world."

"Surely," the seeker thought, "there is a more effective way than that." And so the seeker left that teacher and found another and another and another and many more.

The seeker passed thirty years in the search. Finally the seeker came to a garden. There in the middle of it stood the Tree of Heaven and from its branches hung the bright Fruit of Heaven.

And there, standing beside the Tree, was the first teacher.

"Why did you not tell me when we first met that you yourself were the Custodian of the Fruit of Heaven?" the seeker asked.

"Because," the Teacher said, "you would not have believed me then. And besides, this tree produces fruit only once every thirty years and thirty days."

There is no quick and easy way to make the life of God the life we lead. It takes years of sacred reading, years of listening to all of life, years of learning to listen through the filter of what we have read. A generation of Pop Tarts and instant cocoa and TV dinners and computer calculations and Xerox copies does not prepare us for the slow and tedious task of listening and learning, over and over, day after day, until we can finally hear the people we love and love the people we've learned to dislike and grow to understand how holiness is here and now for us. But someday, in thirty years and thirty days perhaps, we may have listened enough to be ready to gather the yield that comes from years of learning Christ in time, or at least, in the words of the Rule of Benedict, to have made "a good beginning."

Until then, the monastery bells ring out patiently, patiently to remind us to listen. Just listen. Keep listening.

3

Prayer and *Lectio*: The Center and Centrifuge of Life

Whenever we want to ask some favor of a powerful person, we do it humbly and respectfully, for fear of presumption. How much more important, then, to lay our petitions before the God of all things with the utmost humility and sincere devotion. We must know that God regards our purity of heart and tears of compunction, not our many words. Prayer should, therefore, be short and pure, unless perhaps it is prolonged under the inspiration of divine grace.

RB 20:1—4

On the vigils of Sundays and great feasts, our monastery chapel fills with incense as the community prays. The incense wraps around the acolyte who carries it ceremoniously down the aisle as Vespers begins. It pours out of the censer at the base of the altar during the recitation of the Psalms. It wafts around the candles during the reading of the Scripture. By the end of the prayer, it disappears quietly into the cathedral ceiling above and by the time the community has come to the chanting of the "Magnificat," the aura has disappeared entirely. Hardly the scent remains. Whatever it was all intended for, apparently, done. Finished. Gone.

And what was all that incense about? Not mystification surely: the chapel is the chapel, incense or no incense. Not heat: the coals that heat the incense do no more than heat the incense itself. Not antiquity: we have created too modern a setting to let ourselves be fooled that we are functioning in the same style and environment as monastics fifteen centuries before us. No, clearly, the incense on feast days and Sundays must be meant to do something else.

The incense that drenches the community in a filmy heaviness once a week is another kind of reminder of the other-sidedness of prayer. Prayer, the incense says, is not an exercise in recitation. Prayer is the filter through which we view our worlds. Prayer provokes us to see the life around us in fresh, new ways. Prayer is what is left of life after the incense has disappeared. Ancient monastics put it this way:

> "Help us to find God," the disciples asked the elder.
> "No one can help you do that," the elder said.
> "Why not?" the disciples asked amazed.
> "For the same reason that no one can help fish to find the ocean."

Benedictine prayer is not designed to take people out of the world to find God. Benedictine prayer is designed to enable people to realize that God is in the world around them.

Like the incense in the monastic chapel, prayer is meant to call us back to a consciousness of God here and now, not to make God some kind of private getaway from life. On the contrary. Prayer in the Benedictine tradition is a community act and an act of community awareness.

Benedictine prayer, rooted in the Psalms and other Scriptures, takes us out of ourselves to form in us a larger vision of life than we ourselves can ever dredge up out of our own lives alone. Benedictine prayer puts us in contact with past and future at once so that the present becomes clearer and the future possible.

When I was a young monastic, I found prayer a long boring interruption of life. It was not anything the spiritual books and biographies of the period promised it would be. It was not sweet. It did not give me personal consolation. It simply cluttered the day with annoying distractions. Surely my work with students was more important than running in and out of chapel for group recitations of prayers that had nothing whatsoever to do with me or what I was doing at the time. Where were the lights? Where were the insights? Where were the lovely visions of God reported by the saints, assumed by the public, and expected by the spiritually immature? Little by little, I learned.

Benedictine prayer has several characteristics that make more for a spirituality of awareness than of consolation. It is regular. It is universal. It is converting. It is reflective. And it is communal. Out of those qualities a whole new life emerges and people are changed. Not in the way tornadoes change things, perhaps, but in the way that the sand in oysters does.

Prayer that is regular confounds both self-importance and the wiles of the world. It is so easy for good people to confuse their own work with the work of creation. It is so easy to come to believe that what we do is so much more important than what we are. It is so easy to simply get too busy to grow. It is so easy to commit ourselves to this century's demand for product and action until the product consumes us and the actions exhaust us and we can no longer even remember why we set out to do them in the first place.

But regularity in prayer cures all that. Regularity harnesses us to our place in the universe. Morning and evening, season by season, year after year we watch the sun rise and set, death and resurrection daily come and go, beginnings and endings follow one another without terror and without woe. We come to realize that we are simply small parts of a continuing creation, and we take hope and comfort and perspective from that. If getting this contract is all that the world is about; if washing the children's school clothes is the center and the acme of my life; if holding this meeting or getting this promotion or making this money is all that claims my whole life's concentration and fills my whole life's time, then I have become more of a thing than a person and life is really passing me by. Or, I am passing it by.

Benedict called for prayer at regular intervals of each day, right in the middle of apparently urgent and important work. The message is unequivocal. Let no one forget what they are really about. Let no one forget why they have really come to this life. Let no one forget the purpose of life. Let no one forget to remember. Ever. Benedictine spirituality is not a spirituality of escape; Benedictine spirituality is a spirituality that fills time with an awareness of the presence of God.

"Pray always," Scripture says. "Prefer nothing whatsoever to the Work of God" (RB 43:3), the Rule insists. "Impossible," we object. And yet, if we keep our souls tied to a consciousness of God as the Rule directs, even in the face of things of apparently greater or more immediate value, then consciousness of God becomes a given. And consciousness of God is perpetual prayer.

To pray in the midst of the mundane is simply and strongly to assert that this dull and tiring day is holy and its simple labors are the stuff of God's saving presence for me now. To pray simply because it is prayer time is no small act of immersion in the God who is willing to wait for us to be conscious, to be ready, to be willing to become new in life.

Prayer, Benedictine spirituality demonstrates, is not a matter of mood. To pray only when we feel like it is more to seek consolation than to risk conversion. To pray only when it suits us is to want God on our terms. To pray only when it is convenient is to make the God-life a very low priority in a list of better opportunities. To pray only when it feels good is to court total emptiness when we most need to be filled. The hard fact is that nobody finds time for prayer. The time must be taken. There will always be something more pressing to do, something more important to be about than the apparently fruitless, empty act of prayer. But when that attitude takes over, we have begun the last trip down a very short road because, without prayer, the energy for the rest of life runs down. The fuel runs out. We become our own worst enemies: we call ourselves too tired and too busy to pray when, in reality, we are too tired and too busy not to pray. Eventually, the burdens of the day wear us down and we no longer remember why we decided to do what we're doing: work for this project, marry this woman, have these children, minister in this place. And if I cannot remember why I decided to do this, I cannot figure out how I can go on with it. I am tired and the vision just gets dimmer and dimmer.

To pray when we cannot, on the other hand, is to let God be our prayer. The spirituality of regularity requires that we turn over our bruised and bleeding and fragmented and distracted selves to the possibility of conversion, in memory and in hope, in good times and in bad, day after day after day, morning and night, this year and next.

But regularity is not the only call to otherness in Benedictine prayer. Just as the incense drifts out of our hands at solemn vespers so does the notion of prayer as personal panacea disappear quickly once we have lived a Benedictine spirituality for awhile. Benedictine prayer is based almost totally in the Psalms and in the Scriptures. "Let us set out on this way," the Rule reads, "with the Gospel as our guide" (RB Prologue:9). Benedictine prayer, consequently, is not centered in the needs and wants and insights of the person who is praying. It is anchored in the needs and wants and insights of the entire universe. Benedictine prayer pries me out of myself and stretches me beyond myself so that I can come someday, perhaps, to be my best self.

The Scriptures call us to put on the mind of Christ. The Psalms pray out of the struggles of the Psalmist in search of God, out of the struggles of a people in search of life, and out of a consciousness of the cosmic and the universal. Praying the Psalms and the Scriptures, I see with the eyes of Christ, celebrate God in creation, grapple with my own emotional immaturity as the Psalmist did, insert myself into the struggles of the whole people of God.

Under this bright light of broadened human consciousness, I come to realize I am not the center of the

universe but I am cut from its cloth and subject to its
struggles and promised its promises. I learn that prayer
expands my horizons, not enwombs them. I find I bring
to the microscope of prayer not simply the mood of the
moment but the whole life task of becoming fully human.
A Benedictine spirituality that is rooted in the Scriptures
plunges a person into the feelings and forces of the entire
cosmos and brings us up bigger than ourselves.

Benedictine prayer life, besides being scriptural and
regular, is reflective. It is designed to make us take our
own lives into account in the light of the gospel. It is not
recitation for its own sake. It is the bringing to bear of
the mind of Christ on the fragments of our own lives. It
requires steady wrestling with the Word of God. It takes
time and it does not depend on quantity for its value.

Not so long ago, though, a prayer-wheel mentality of
the spiritual life was beginning to eat away at monastic
communities too. Like the industrialized world around
them, where assembly lines had become the model of
life's best operations, the notion that more is better invaded the churches and the monasteries with a ven-
geance. Novenas followed holy days that followed the sea-
sons of the church, that followed the private devotions
that followed the multiplication of Eucharists. We prayed
prayers and prayed prayers and prayed prayers.

To the agricultural culture of time and season, we
added the industrial culture of unending shifts and fren-
zied production. Soon the practice of seven different periods of daily prayer was compounded by a whole range
of full-time ministries. And prayer got longer and faster
and more mechanical all the time. In a simpler society,
Benedict had called for regular prayer punctuated by long

periods of sacred reading and equal measures of meaningful work. Our culture, though, turned the spiritual life
into a more-is-better world and was fast losing the value
of any and all of it.

Prayer, work, and holy leisure are the three legs that
support the spiritual foundation of Benedictinism. Each
one is meant to complement the other. Not one of the
three is to be abandoned. Prayer makes us conscious of
the presence of God, work makes us co-creators of the
Kingdom, holy leisure gives us time for the reflective
reading of Scripture that makes prayer a real experience
rather than the recitation of formulas. Reflective reading
of Scripture is what draws me into the text and the text
into my life. Like the Chosen People, I discover by plumb-
ing the text, I have been on an exodus of my own and
raised my own questions in the face of God and grumbled
about my life circumstances and danced in front of idols
called my career or my self or my wants. Like Eli I have
tolerated evil in the world and never said a word. Like
Esther I have convinced myself that I have no responsibility for the destruction of whole peoples by my own
government. The Benedictine tradition of *lectio*, or reflective reading of the sacred books, calls me to take my
place among these figures who were called to work out
their salvation, as I am, in a world that waits to be re-
minded by someone of the eternal will of God.

Benedictine prayer calls for more than prayer time; it
calls for attention to the Scriptures. It calls for more than
words; it calls for a change of mind and values. It calls
for more than ritual; it calls for deep reflection. It calls
for more than getting my prayers in; it requires that I get
my heart steeped in the story of God in history.

The prayer life that comes from regularity, reflection,

and a sense of the universal, however, is very soon converting. The function of prayer is certainly not to cajole God into saving us from ourselves. "Please, God, don't let us die in nuclear war" surely is not real prayer. We can stop nuclear war ourselves by stopping the manufacture of nuclear weapons. Humans created them and humans can destroy them. No, the function of prayer is not magic. The function of prayer is not the bribery of the Infinite. The function of prayer is not to change the mind of God about decisions we have already made for ourselves.

The function of prayer is to change my own mind, to put on the mind of Christ, to enable grace to break into me. When prayer is privatized religion on a spree, it's not prayer. Contemplative prayer, converting prayer, is prayer that sees the whole world through incense—a holy place, a place where the sacred dwells, a place to be made different by those who pray, a place where God sweetens living with the beauty of all life. Contemplative prayer is prayer that leads us to see our world through the eyes of God. It unstops our ears to hear the poverty of widows, the loneliness of widowers, the cry of women, the vulnerability of children, the struggle of outcasts, the humanity of enemies, the insights of the uneducated, the tensions of bureaucrats, the fears of rulers, the wisdom of the holy, the power of the powerless.

Prayer leads us and leavens us and enlightens us. And changes us. It makes us something bigger than we are.

Finally, Benedictine prayer is communal. Benedictine prayer is prayer with a community and for a community and as a community. It is commitment to a pilgrim people whose insights grow with time and whose needs are common to us all. Community prayer in the Benedictine tradition is a constant reminder that we do not go to church for ourselves alone. It is a chosen people, a human race, a body of faithful who stand in witness, first to one another, that God is God. And yet it is not that there is no room for the self here. It is just that the self grows best when self is not its end. To say, "I have a good prayer life, I don't need to go to church" or "I don't get anything out of prayer" is to admit our paucity, either on the communal or the personal level.

In fact, the problem may be that as a church we have done entirely too much with private Eucharists in the immediate past and far too little with common prayer. Gone are the days of parish vespers and parish retreats and parish missions. Individualism has infected even the churches. We find God alone and so we make God in our own image and likeness. And then we make our life decisions in the same way. We do what is good for us, as individuals, as business people, as nations. We even pray for what is good for us and miss the witness and needs of the handicapped and the poor and the disenfranchised and the marginal and the alienated and the lonely.

But community prayer is meant to bind us to one another and to broaden our vision of the needs of the world and to give us models to steer by and friends to uphold us and encourage us and enable us to go on. The praying community becomes the vehicle for my own fidelity. Because they are there praying, I go to prayer. Because they are there always, I make room in my life for them and for God. Because they are there consistently, I can never put them and their witness and their needs out of my mind. Private prayer, Benedict says, may follow communal prayer, but it can never substitute for it. Prayer, in fact, forms the community mind.

The implications of all these qualities for contemporary spirituality are plain:

- God is to be dialogued with in the Word daily—not simply attended to at times of emotional spasm—until little by little the gospel begins to work in me. Prayer must be scriptural, not simply personal.
- Time for prayer must be set aside and kept: after the children go to school; before breakfast in the morning; in the car on the way to work; on the bus coming home; at night before going to bed.
- Reflection on the Scriptures is basic to growth in prayer and to growth as a person. Prayer is a process of coming to be something new. It is not simply a series of exercises.
- Understanding is essential to the act of prayer. Formulas are not enough.
- Changes in attitudes and behaviors are a direct outcome of prayer. Anything else is more therapeutic massage than confrontation with God.
- A sense of community is both the bedrock and the culmination of prayer. I pray to become a better human being, not to become better at praying.

"There are three stages of spiritual development," a teacher taught. "The carnal, the spiritual, and the divine."

"What is the carnal stage?" the disciple asked.

"That's the stage," the teacher said, "when trees are seen as trees and mountains are seen as mountains."

"And the spiritual?" the disciple asked eagerly.

"That's when we look more deeply into things. Then trees

are no longer trees and mountains are no longer mountains," the teacher answered.

"And the divine?" the disciple said breathlessly.

"Ah," the teacher said with a smile. "That's Enlightenment—when the trees become trees again and the mountains become mountains."

We pray to see life as it is, to understand it, and to make it better than it was. We pray so that reality can break into our souls and give us back our awareness of the Divine Presence in life. We pray to understand things as they are, not to ignore and avoid and deny them.

We pray so that when the incense disappears we can still see the world as holy.

4

Community: The Basis of Human Relationships

This, then, is the good zeal which monastics must foster with fervent love: "They should each try to be the first to show respect to the other" (Rom. 12:10), supporting with the greatest patience one another's weakness of body or behavior, and earnestly competing in obedience to one another. No one is to pursue what is judged better for self, but instead what is judged better for someone else. To their companions they show the pure love of sisters or brothers; to God, loving fear; to their abbot, unfeigned and humble love. Let them prefer nothing whatever to Christ, and may Christ bring us all together to everlasting life.

RB 72:3–11

There are icons of Benedict and Scholastica that hang in the chapel foyer of our monastery. There are oil paintings and wood mosaics of them in every hall and public room. There are statues of them in the library and on the lawn facing the road that runs along the property outside. They are everywhere. And every one of those figures, no matter what the medium, says just one thing to me about them: Human. Very human.

For all the centuries of art that have depicted them, the portraitures of Benedict and Scholastica have been saved somehow from the distortions of romanticism. They are not bigger than life. They are not set in shining halos. They are not surrounded by angels. Only one characteristic outdoes the rest: they both have piercing eyes.

Sight and humanity are, I think, the basic gifts of Benedictine community. The ability to see is both a strength and a weakness. If we learn to see life as it is instead of as we want it to be, we have an edge on happiness. More likely, though, we set out to shape life according to our own image and likeness.

The Rule of Benedict simply laughs at the idea. Benedict doesn't set up a model of rarefied existence as the end of the spiritual life. Benedict sets up a community, a family. And families, the honest among us will admit, are risky places to be if perfection is what you are expecting in life.

Of all the places where the Rule of Benedict departs from the traditional norms of religious life, it is surely in its theology of community. And of all the places where the Rule of Benedict shows us the real depth of the spiritual life, it is surely in its theology of community. "The most valiant kind of monk," Benedict writes in a culture of hermits, is not the solitary or the pseudoascetic or the wandering beggar but "the cenobite" (RB 1:12), the one who has learned to live with others in community. In fact, the gift of Benedictine spirituality to the modern world may well be community itself.

The desert ascetics before him had been disciplined, other-worldly solitaries whose sole work of life was concentration on God. Benedictine monastics, on the other hand, were ordinary people whose whole work of life was concentration on God and service to one another. But who doesn't know after a long, hard day of meeting people and listening to people and cleaning up after people how inviting a desert can be. In the desert surely, God would talk directly to us. In the community, God speaks too, but only through the others. Ah, yes, people say, I would love to go to a monastery to get away from this mortgage and this wild child and this pressure and this sloppy wife and this demanding husband and this corporate rat race and these sponging relatives. Hold it. Not so fast. The monastery will not offer an escape from all of this, but it might offer a model for dealing with them.

Exactly what do the eyes of Benedict and Scholastica see when they look at the human community? First, the Rule is clear: love costs. It costs the little daily things— serving the meals, providing the needs, asking for favors nicely, refusing favors gently. Second, love makes demands. It demands that we use our gifts for our own communities as well as for others. It demands that we make relationships a priority. It demands that we make community for others. It demands that we share ourselves, our minds, our insights, and our time with one another. Most of all, it demands that we allow the people in our lives to be who they are and grow as they can.

Community is the only antidote we have to an individualism that is fast approaching the heights of the pathological and the sinful in this world. Folk literature gives us a very insightful glimpse of a growing world problem. In the Far East there is a traditional image of the difference between heaven and hell. In hell, the ancients said, people have chopsticks one yard long so they cannot possibly reach their mouths. In heaven, the chopsticks are also one yard long—but, in heaven, the people feed one another.

It is not a case, in other words, of what we have in life. It is a case of what we do with it that determines the quality of the communal life we lead.

Benedictine spirituality is intent on the distribution of self for the sake of the other. But it is intent as well on the presence of the other for my sake as well.

In this model of life, unlike the standard-brand American dream, it isn't that every person in a family has a car that makes or breaks good family life. It is a matter of how the cars they do have are shared among them that measures the health and love of that group. In this vision of life, it isn't that women in a family pour themselves out for their families and friends, their neighborhoods and nations; it is that not only the women be expected to pour themselves out if real family, real community, real relationships are to be achieved. In this schema, it isn't only the man of the family who works to support it, but everyone is expected to contribute to the health and future of the group.

Indeed, the vision of human community that shines in the eyes of the icons of Benedict and Scholastica is a very different model from the one we see around us in our culture today. There are qualities common to community life in the Rule of Benedict that are sadly missing from modern society. And in their stead we reap alienation and self-centeredness and calculated cosmic ruin.

The Benedictine spirituality of community is based on life with other persons in the spirit of Christ: to support them, to empower them, and to learn from them. The radical monastic testimony of this commitment to universal human love is celibacy, the public declaration that the monastic will belong to everyone and to no one at the same time. Celibacy says that human community is built on a great deal more than the sexual, that it transcends sexual love, and pours itself out with no expectation of outpouring in return. Community, the Rule reminds us, is to be built on "chaste" love, on love that does not use or exploit the other, on love that can give without requiring equal payment in return, on love that is not based on the gratification of the self. And that is exactly why the Benedictine spirituality of community is not for celibates alone.

In a culture in which sex has become a consuming issue, a national passion, an underlying current in every social stream, Benedictine spirituality calls for love in breadth and love in depth and love in human, rather than simply sexual, terms. The spirituality of celibacy says that each of us is whole before God, that God has absolute priority for us, that God is sufficient for us, and that God's demands over our lives are total. The married, the single, and the monastic all have this same call to ultimate aloneness and ultimate union with God, and eventually every life will bow to it. Monastics only draw the call in clearer, broader, bolder lines here so the whole world can see its reality.

Interestingly enough, though, even in monasticism celibacy has often been reduced to the sexual. As a young woman in community, I was not even permitted to ride in the front seat of the car when I was alone with my father. Old spiritual reading books counseled us not to pick up small children so that we wouldn't jeopardize our vocations. We concentrated more on keeping our distance than on widening our grasp on the world. Real monastic celibacy, though, is human love that points to a greater love. Real monastic celibacy challenges the sexual chaos of our time to something beyond the sensual that ebbs and flows throughout our time to the spiritual that lasts forever. To live totally in God and totally for others can be a counterweight of value to an extremely self-centered world.

Benedict's spirituality of community is based first of all on bondedness in Christ. Neither communities nor families exist for themselves alone. They exist to witness to Christ and in Christ. They exist to be miracle worker to one another. They exist to make the world the family it is meant to be. Their purpose is to draw us always into the center of life where values count and meaning matters more than our careers or our personal convenience.

The fact is that simply living with people does not by itself create community. People live together in armies and prisons and college dormitories and hospitals, but they are not communities unless they live out of the same reservoir of values and the same center of love. Marrying the rich husband or the proper wife, going to religious life to avoid responsibility rather than to respond to it has nothing to do with bondedness in Christ. We have to share a common vision. We have to want good for one another. We have to be able to draw from the same well together. "Let us open our eyes to the light that comes from God, and our ears to the voice from heaven," the Rule says (RB Prologue:9).

So, even liking one another is not enough. The truth about Christian community is that we have to be committed to the same eternal things together. What we want to live for and how we intend to live out those values are the central questions of community. Without that understanding, communities fail and marriages dissolve and people leave religious life and nations go to war.

Another function of community is to enable us to be about something greater than ourselves. It is no small task in a world that tells us constantly that we ourselves are enough to be concerned about and that everything else will take care of itself. Well, that kind of enlightened altruism has not saved us from the destruction of the ozone layer, or the deterioration of the centers of our cities, or massive unemployment even among educated upper-middle-class executives, or wars against the innocent on every front.

The truth is that, as a people, we simply have not cultivated in our time the spiritual commitment to pay attention to life beyond our own backyards. We take care of us and nothing else because no greater vision of life impels us and because we lack the sense of human community that requires us to be for others. Every ad agency in the country sells us personal satisfaction, not group growth. We learn early to do our own thing. We discover very young in this culture to look out for "ol' number one." The notion of doing something because it benefits others sells very little in this world.

Into this milieu, Benedictine spirituality inserts a consciousness of life together in Christ, not simply life that is convenient for me. Those who look to a spirit of Benedictine community life as a model for their own must be grounded in Christ and intent on becoming a sign of the power of Christian community to others.

It isn't that members of a Benedictine community don't have lives of their own. It is simply that to the monastic, life without the others is only half a life. Life without the community of faith leaves us without a sense of more than us in life, and that is a barren life at best. When we transcend ourselves for the other, though, community becomes the sacrament of human fulfillment and purpose in life.

A Benedictine spirituality of community, therefore, has a reverence for uniqueness as well as bondedness. Conformity is not the end of Benedictine life; it is community of heart and soul and mind toward which we move, not control. But to understand that is to free us from having to control everyone in our world and it is to free them from enslavement to our egos.

Possessiveness goes when uniqueness in community is understood. We begin to realize that the gift of the individuals in our lives must be given as God gave them, freely and recklessly. We begin to realize that we don't have the master plan for everybody else's life. We begin to see that children must be allowed to go their own way and that husbands have to be allowed to make their dreams come true instead of simply making their bank accounts bigger and wives must be permitted to become gifted people themselves instead of simply being the family's live-in help.

We begin to learn to trust our own gifts, too, but not for their own sake. We develop our gifts in the Benedictine tradition when we use them for the good of others. Let the artists work at their crafts, the Rule says, "and let them sell their goods for less" (RB 57:8). Our gifts are to be given away so that the whole human community is richer for our having been here.

In Benedictine spirituality, community is a very human thing. We do not expect perfection here, but we do expect growth, in ourselves as well as in others. Here everyone holds a privileged place, whatever their place. In Benedict's community, slave and free were equals; priests and lay were equals; old and young were equals. Each had a say and each gifts and each had needs and each had obligations to the others.

In a mentality of family equality, fathers do not have a right to rage at their families and children do not have a right to tyrannize the household and mothers do not have a right to withhold their mothering on the grounds that they are people too. But each of them does have a right to be listened to and given help when life's tasks are too much for them to manage without help. "Let help be given where it is needed" (RB 53:20), the Rule instructs. The function of family, in other words, is not to establish roles. The function of family is to establish the family.

Community goes astray, consequently, when it begins to be seen simply as a jumping-off point for our own personal ambitions instead of an arena in which I am meant to give my gifts to the rest of the human race so that we can all live better together. When I begin to think that my community owes me this or my family doesn't love me unless they give me that, or my friends have to change their plans for mine, then I am clearly intent on creating a world unto myself, not a community. When her career and his ambitions and their laziness become the pivot around which these relationships begin to operate, we don't have community at all. We have a privatization of the Garden of Eden.

It was the sight of everybody, old and young, sophisticated and simple, administrators and staff, scrubbing woodwork and sweeping steps and washing walls that most affected me as a young monastic. It is the sight of everyone taking a turn at table-waiting at community meals and everyone at choir practice and everyone doing dishes and everyone setting up the dining room tables for great feast days and everyone doing the Christmas decorating together and everyone packing boxes for the community giveaway days that most makes me realize that we are all in this together. Then I know in a special way that I am not alone. Then I realize with new insight that there are basics in life more important than a business schedule. Then I understand that those basics are love of God and fun and companionship on the long, dark roads of life and partnership in the great human enterprise. We have to learn to be for one another so that the love of God is a shining certainty, even now, even here. That is the function and the blessing of community. And it is a far cry from the rugged individualism, the narcissism, and the brutal independence that has become the insulation in our neighborhoods and the hallmark of our culture.

Finally, the Benedictine spirituality of community depends on stability, on seeing things through, on working things out, on going on. Everything in life, contrary to Madison Avenue's guarantees, can't be cured or resolved or eliminated. Some things must simply be endured. Some things must simply be borne. Some things must simply be accepted. Community and relationships enable us to do that. Community and relationships are meant to hold us up on the days when we are very, very down.

In community we work out our connectedness to God, to one another, and to ourselves. It is in community where we find out who we really are. It is life with another that shows my impatience and life with another that demonstrates my possessiveness and life with another that gives notice to my nagging devotion to the self. Life with someone else, in other words, doesn't show me nearly as much about his or her shortcomings as it does about my own. In human relationships I learn how to soften my hard spots and how to reconcile and how to care for someone else besides myself. In human relationships I learn that theory is no substitute for love. It is easy to talk about the love of God; it is another thing to practice it.

That's how relationships sanctify me. They show me where holiness is for me. That's how relationships develop me. They show me where growth is for me. If I'm the passive-victim type, then assertiveness may have something to do with coming to wholeness. If I'm the domineering character in every group, then a willingness to listen and to be led may be my call to life. Alone, I am what I am, but in community I have the chance to become everything that I can be.

And so, stability bonds me to this group of people and to these relationships so that resting in the security of each other we can afford to stumble and search, knowing that we will be caught if we fall and we will be led where we cannot see by those who have been there before us. In a Benedictine community, all ages live side by side, the young with the old, the well with the infirm, and each learns from the other. The elderly learn from the young that life goes on, that creation keeps creating. The young learn from the elderly that life is about more than titles and careers, that someday we shall each be only what we are and no more. Then, we will all look back on our relationships with God, with our selves, and with others as the only lasting mark of our humanity.

"Whose feet shall the hermit wash?" Basil, from whom Benedict drew much of his own inspiration, asked centuries ago. The question needs to be asked again in a culture devoted largely to the worship of itself. Unless we learn in our own personal relationships, as the ancient definition of heaven and hell indicates, to live for someone besides ourselves, how shall we as a nation ever learn to hear the cries of the starving in Ethiopia and the illiterate in Africa and the refugees in the Middle East and the war weary in Central America? What will become of a nation in this day and age that has no sense of community? What, indeed, will become of the planet? The warning of the wise is clear:

"In hell," the Vietnamese write, "the people have chopsticks but they are three feet long so that they cannot reach their mouths. In Heaven the chopsticks are the same length, but in heaven the people feed one another." The message is no less new, no less important today.

The very human, very piercing eyes of Benedict and Scholastica see all of that and leave us with life-giving choices to make. Community is our only option.

5

Humility: The Lost Virtue

[I]f we want to reach the highest summit of humility, if we desire to attain speedily that exaltation in heaven to which we climb by the humility of this present life, then by our ascending actions we must set up that ladder on which Jacob in a dream saw "angels descending and ascending" (Gen. 28:12). Without doubt, this descent and ascent can signify only that we descend by exaltation and ascend by humility. Now the ladder erected is our life on earth, and, if we humble our hearts, God will raise it to heaven. We may call our body and soul the sides of this ladder, into which our divine vocation has fitted the various steps of humility and discipline as we ascend.

RB 7:5–10

One of the most interesting spots in our monastery is its inner courtyard. Exotic flowers grow there in every season and very few people notice them. Most of the windows that border the courtyard belong to private workspaces. The few public vantage points are in narrow corridors where people need to keep moving by rather than being able to gather and look. Yet, the courtyard is one of the most life-giving places we have. It gives light to the inside of the monastery. It breeds beauty. Much like a Japanese garden, it centers the house in peace. And everybody knows it. And few people see it. But without it the house would be a completely different place.

Benedict does that with his chapter on humility. He places it inconspicuously in the center of the Rule, and it leavens the entire document, the entire way of life.

Humility is not an easy thing to talk about in the twentieth century. Nor was it in the sixth century, I'm sure. Patriarchy was an institution of divine right. Slave and free were sharply divided. Roman citizenship was the passport to the good life. There was no room for humility here and little tolerance for it either.

In our own generation, humility has at best been labeled neurotic. It is self-esteem and personal growth and getting ahead that we're all about. If humility has something to do with being passive, meek, and self-effacing, those are not qualities that we call healthy, let alone smart. And I admit that humility as it has been presented has certainly left things to be desired.

In our novitiate, humility was interpreted as not being noticed, not speaking up, not questioning the questionable, not advancing our own gifts. We were not, after all, too far away yet from the age when the watering of sticks was used to prove the monastic's ability to take ridiculous orders without arrogant resistance. I never did understand all that too well. The people I knew and admired most were all very effective people who knew it and who kept getting better at it. I was convinced, moreover, that they were also humble. I just couldn't say, though, how I knew that to be so. Then I studied the Rule.

The twentieth century has plenty to relearn about humility and the Rule of Benedict may be its best model. Benedict identifies twelve degrees of humility, twelve levels of personal growth that lead to peace. They lead to other things too. They lead to self-development and they lead to community consciousness. Like our courtyard, they permeate all of life, quietly and unobtrusively and totally. The fact is that everyone has something that controls his or her entire life. For some, it's ambition; for some, it's greed; for some, it's dependence; for some, it's fear; for some, it's self-centeredness. Benedict wants us to permeate our lives with reality. Monastics of another age put it this way:

One day the Teacher said, "It is so much easier to travel than to stop."

"Why?" the disciples demanded to know.

"Because," the Teacher said, "as long as you travel to a goal you can hold on to a dream. When you stop, you must face reality."

"But how shall we ever change if we have no goals or dreams?" the disciples asked.

"Change that is real is change that is not willed. Face reality and unwilled change will happen."

Humility is reality to the full.

Benedict couches his teachings on humility in six basic principles. With these understandings it is clear that Benedict's definition of humility and the use of the term in the twentieth century are light years apart.

In the first place, Benedictine spirituality implies, the presence of God demands total response. If I really believe God is present in my life, here and now, then I have no choice but to deal with that. Life, in fact, will not be resolved for me until I do. No manner of other agendas will ever completely smother the insistency of the God one. No amount of noise will ever successfully drown out the need to discover what is most important among all the important things of life. No degree of success will ever feel like success until I am succeeding at the center point of life.

Second, the Rule makes clear, the pride that is the opposite of humility is not the excitement that comes with doing well what I do best. The pride that is the opposite of monastic humility is the desire to be my own God and to control other people and other things. It is not pride to enjoy my achievements. That kind of awareness is the spirit of the "Magnificat" at its height. It is pride to want to wrench my world and all the people in it to my ends. It is arrogance to the utmost to insist that other people shape their lives to make mine comfortable. It is arrogance unabashed to think that God must do the same.

The third basic principle of monastic humility is that spiritual development is a process. If the spirituality of the immediate past is tainted by anything at all, it is the notion that growth is an event. People who graduated from high school were considered grown-up. People who got married were said to be grown-up. People who became parents were automatically grown-up. People who went to monasteries and seminaries were undoubtedly grown-up. And we treated the spiritual life the same way. We put people through a series of spiritual gymnastics and assumed if they did certain things certain ways, that in itself was proof of spiritual progress. To walk with downcast eyes was prayerful. To climb up the cathedral steps on your knees, I had been told as a child, was a sign of repentance. To take the last place in line if you were a priest was humble. But nothing is more insidious than spiritual pride; nothing is more impervious to identification. No, the monastic mind-set says, spiritual development is not an event. Spiritual development is a process of continuing conversion. "What do you do in the monastery?" an ancient tale asks. "Oh, we fall and we get up. We fall and we get up," the old monastic answers. In monastic spirituality, we never arrive; we are always arriving.

In Benedictine spirituality, too, humility and humiliations are two distinct concepts, and they are not necessarily related. The Rule does not call for humiliations. The Rule calls for the humility it would take to deal with the humiliating aspects of life and come out of them psychologically well and spiritually sound. It is possible, in other words, to live our whole life in a series of humiliations and know nothing about humility. Humiliation may teach us a lot about oppression, or a lot about underdevelopment or a great deal about anger, but it will not necessarily prove that we have learned anything about humility. Benedictine humility frees the spirit; it does not batter it.

Humility, the Rule implies, is the glue of our relationships. Humility is the foundation of community and family and friendship and love. Humility comes from understanding my place in the universe.

Finally, the Rule shows us, self-love is destructive of self. If we allow an unwarranted, unlimited kind of self-concern to consume us, our very mental health is in question.

In 1980, so corrosive had the effects of exaggerated self-importance become that the American Psychiatric Association began to identify narcissism as a personality disorder. Clearly, the cultural effects of rampant individualism have come home to haunt us. The symptoms of narcissism, the professionals agree, that are signs of an unintegrated personality include a grandiose and exaggerated sense of self-importance; preoccupation with fantasies of success; exhibitionism and insatiable attention-getting maneuvers; disdain or disproportionate rage in the face of criticism; a sense of entitlement that undermines any hope for success in personal relationships; talk that is more self-promotion than communication (Millon, Theodore. *Disorders of Personality.* New York: John Wiley & Sons, 1981). The Rule of Benedict reads like a therapeutic regimen against the illness.

In a culture where the individual is always considered more important than the group and family tensions arise over whose agenda shall become the basis of the home, it is often difficult to know when personal needs have become exploitative. But someplace between these poles of extreme suppression and extreme selfishness, monastic humility provides a basis for human community and a basis for union with God.

To Benedict the process is clearly the work of a lifetime. He calls it "a ladder of humility" (RB 7:6), a climb with basic parts, a progression—not a leap—that involves the integration of both body and soul. "Our body and our soul are the two sides of this ladder" (RB 7:9), he teaches. No dualism here, just the simple, honest admission that each of us is grounded in something but reaching for God and that each of us is attempting to bring the demands of the body and the hope of the soul into parallel, into harmony, into center. Against gravity and despite all the imbalances of our lives. Pulling body and soul together is the problem. It is also the project of life.

The tower and ladder symbols were favorites with the ancients, but it was left to Augustine to give us that marvelous line: "Do you seek God? Seek within yourself and ascend through yourself." If we are really seeking God, we have to start in the very core of our own hearts and motives and expectations. We can't blame the schedule or the finances or the work or the people in our lives for blocking our progress. We have to learn to seek from within ourselves. We have to stop waiting for the world around us to be perfect in order to be happy.

Then, however, Benedict does a totally countercultural thing with his ladder image. He turns it upside down: "We descend by exaltation," he says, and "we ascend by humility" (RB 7:7). The monastic life, it seems, has different values from the values of life around it. To set out on the path of Benedictine spirituality is to see the world differently from the way it is seen by those around us. What they call up, we may well call down. What they call success we may well call failure. What they call achievement we may well call entrapment. We aren't in this thing for ourselves only. We're going to God by pouring ourselves out in a culture that hoards money and titles and invitations and power like gold.

For here in the presentation of humility, life is put before us raw. Here life is simply life. Here life by current standards is totally reversed: up is indeed down; humility is exaltation. Life is not about "me." Life is about God. What the psychiatrists have begun to hint at, Benedict already knew. Self-preference, self-will, self-love, and radical egotism are attempts to make ourselves our God. I become the ultimate arbiter of good and evil in my life. Growth becomes impossible.

Benedict's process for achieving humility and conversion in life is outlined in twelve progressive degrees, each one essential to the achievement of the next and each one a simple excursion into accepting life in the here and now as the refiner's fire of my present and the raw material of my future. It is a very simple approach to what we insist on making complex.

"The first degree of humility," the Rule reads, "is that we always have the fear of God before our eyes, shunning all forgetfulness and that we be ever mindful of all that God has commanded" (RB 7:10–11). The first rung of the ladder to union with God and harmony in life is to let God be God. We make so many things in life god—this job, that person, this thing, that title—that eventually we forget who God really is. We forget what really lasts in life. We forget that there are responsibilities that come with creaturehood: to tend the garden and to care for it, to take care of the creatures and to be helpmates to one another. We forget the presence of God and so we act as if God were not present. We belittle one another and make fun of the poor and reject the alien. We make ourselves god and forget the will of God in others for us.

The second degree of humility follows easily. If God is present in life then I must accept the will of God for me. When circumstances persist even though I bend every effort to eliminate them, then clearly those are the will of God for me. There is something in them that I must learn to deal with. There is something about them that is essential to my growth. There are, at least, other ways and other answers and other plans than mine that obviously bear recognition if I am to grow beyond myself and come to appreciate the beauty in others.

The third degree of humility requires that we be willing to subject ourselves to the direction of others. Here we touch the human being's unlimited will to power. Here we're brought to learn that there are events and people outside my life who, like it or not, do have power over me. Here I am asked to acknowledge my mortality.

Life is not in my hands. I am not in control of every aspect of it and it is only when I fool myself into thinking that I am that the frustration sets in.

The recognition of any authority outside myself leashes the insatiable thirst for power within me. Humility means I might be able to listen to the manager at work. It means I might be able to take directions from a friend. It means I might not have to control my home and my schedule and my territory. It means I might be free to give up arrogance and foreswear omnipotence. It means I admit I need conversion and then open myself to seeking and accepting the will of God through others. The fact is that I do not have unlimited freedom. Obedience to God's will sets limits.

The fourth degree of humility brings us to accept the difficulties imposed on us by others in life "with patience and even temper and not grow weary or give up" (RB 7:35–36). This degree of humility asks for emotional maturity. Life is full of hard things, most of which are not impossible and not immoral, simply difficult. Sometime in the spiritual life we have to stop running away from the things that aggravate us so we can see what it is that is being demanded of us that we are refusing to give.

Most of all, the fourth degree of humility requires that we give everybody else's ideas a chance. When we accept people in positions above us, we can't second-guess everything they do or want instant effects. Sometimes we will just have to wait. Sometimes we will just have to keep trying to make the thing work their way. Sometimes we will just have to let the others figure out the weaknesses of a thing in their own way, in their own good time. What good will pushing really do? And what is the good of a better idea about meaningless things if we lose our life relationships in the process of proving ourselves to be right?

"The fifth degree of humility is when one hides from the Abbot none of the evil thoughts that rise in one's heart or the evils committed in secret but humbly confesses them" (RB 7:44). The monastic heart is asked to put down hypocrisy, is asked to quit pretending to be something it is not, is asked to open itself to the cure of souls. What this degree of humility implies an entire profession has arisen to affirm. The psychologist knows that when we throw light into the caves of our hearts we discover without question that the dragon that lives there is not nearly as big as we thought.

This degree says if we want to grow, self-disclosure and interaction with others are imperative. We admit our weaknesses and limitations and someone else—a friend, wife, husband, parent, someone close enough to care about how we develop—guides us through the morass of uncertainties and struggles that our lives have somehow, silently and insidiously, become. Someone holds us up while we go on. We put down all our false images and we become who we are with someone who cares. We recognize someone else's strengths so that they can call us from our weakness.

At the next level of development, the sixth, the monastic is asked to "be content with the meanest and worst of everything" (RB 7:49). Grasping for the fineries of life has become an American obsession. Small children have learned to want the best of the world's racing bikes, not just a bike. Adults have learned that their backyards are incomplete, no matter how beautiful, without a swimming pool of their own. Young college graduates have been conditioned to expect top pay and good restaurants and big cars to come automatically with the diploma. To be seen on a three-speed bike or to swim in the park or to work for a small company where the pay is modest and the office appointments are functional rather than elegant is somehow to have failed. How can it possibly be explained to the neighbors?

In Benedictine spirituality, the explanation is simple: what I need to make me happy in this life is not of this world. I was not put here to have the best of life's goods; I was put here to have what I need for my body so my soul can thrive. I was put here to appreciate what is.

Of all the degrees of humility, the fifth degree of self-disclosure may be the most American and the sixth degree of self-denial the most un-American. Why not have all the things I can have? Because I don't need them, and they clutter the soul and tie me down to the lesser things in life. No time for sacred reading while I clean the pool; no time for the family while I'm climbing the corporate ladder instead of the ladder of humility. No time to discover the basic joys of life when I'm allowed to learn young the need to outstrip the neighborhood in things. No time even to learn the value of money when what I use it for isn't needed at all. But this degree of humility that calls us to be content with less frees us from the cloying burden of the unnecessary in life.

The sixth degree of humility touches to the quick. Is it wrong to buy the larger car? Is it un-Christian to own the beach house? Is it unholy to build well, and buy well, and invest well? And if so, what about the huge monasteries and big churches and great art pieces that are so common a part of Benedictine monasteries themselves? The situation is a delicate one and not to be rationalized. Amassing, hoarding, overbuilding, and overbuying are inimical to Benedictine spirituality. Beauty, simplicity, need, sufficiency, and the just distribution of goods are essential to it. Benedictine spirituality does not call for poverty. Benedictine spirituality calls for right use and generous care and the open hand. There is a thin line between the two, granted, but the line is worth walking and the discomfort is worth bearing if it becomes the criteria we use to measure our own complicity in a society that is never content with the worst of anything, that has to be number one in everything.

The challenge of the sixth degree of humility is to live prophetically in a world that thinks only in terms of getting more rather than of having enough. Benedictine spirituality, real humility, demands that we hold only to give and that we gather only to share.

The seventh degree of humility, presented in the language of the sixth century, is hard to accept on first blush. It reads: "The seventh degree of humility is when the monastic believes that he or she is the lowest and vilest of all" (RB 7:51). But it's equally hard to take when it's reversed: "The seventh degree of humility is when we believe that we are the highest and best of all." And that's the clue to understanding it, I believe. Unless we see ourselves as potentially weaker, potentially more sinful, potentially more confused than anyone around us, how can we possibly understand and accept them? If we make ourselves the norm of society, who else can ever meet our standards? If we see ourselves as Mary of Nazareth instead of Mary Magdalene, more like John than like Judas, then where is the room for conversion in our own lives; where is the room for compassion for others?

It's the seventh degree of humility that requires us to learn to take criticism. It asks us to accept the fact that there is plenty of room for growth in us. Thanks to the seventh degree of humility we can open ourselves to new possibilities within ourselves. Here we stop saying, "Well, that's just the way I am," and begin to say, "There is more that I can be." This seventh degree of humility, then, is the degree of humility that deals with a new perspective on life.

The eighth degree of humility reminds us of our place in the human race. At the eighth degree, the monastic "does nothing but what is sanctioned by the Rule and the example of the elders" (RB 7:55). Benedictine spirituality depends on our being willing to listen and to learn from what perennially has been found to be true. We learn that community itself is a source of wisdom for us, that the major relationships of our lives have not been given to us to be exploited by us; they have been given to us to teach us. We learn we must learn at every stage of life from those who have gone before us. We learn to learn from what has been found trustworthy by others instead of insisting on reinventing every wheel. We learn we are not the center of the universe but there is plenty that we can gain from others at every age. We learn we will never arrive and that is all right.

And, finally, like the psychologists of our own day, Benedict deals with speech. In the ninth, tenth and eleventh degrees of humility, Benedict counsels the disciple to "withhold the tongue from speaking" (RB 7:56), "to be not easily moved and quick for laughter" (RB 7:59), and "to speak gently, humbly, with gravity and with few and sensible words" (RB 7:60).

The focus of the three is apparent: we shouldn't spend our lives telling other people how to run theirs. We should be soft in our speech, not harsh, not hard, not raucous, not rude, not rough. We should not be making light of serious things. We should not be making fun of other people. Life is serious business; acting the buffoon, being superficial about it, eating up our time with things that have no meaning for eternity, going through life under water does not make for the well-lived life.

We should care about important things. We should be attending to things of substance. We should be kind to people. We should be listeners. These three degrees are clearly the way the humble person responds to others: not arrogantly, but reverently. These three degrees are humility's response to others. When we have learned who we are, we can begin to treat others better. For the first time, perhaps, we can see who the others in our lives really are with all their wisdom and all their beauty and all their gifts and all their faces of Christ.

Finally, the Rule teaches us, the twelfth degree of humility is that we are not only humble of heart but always let it appear also in our whole exterior to everyone who sees us.

People who are really humble, who know themselves to be earth or humus—the root from which our word "humble" comes—have about themselves, an air of self-containment and self-control. There's no haughtiness, no distance, no sarcasm, no put downs, no airs of importance or disdain. The ability to deal with both their own limitations and the limitations of others, the recognition that God is in life and that they are not in charge of the universe brings serenity and hope, inner peace and real energy. Humble people walk comfortably in every group. No one is either too beneath them or too above them for their own sense of well-being. They are who they are, people with as much to give as to get, and they know it. And because they're at ease with themselves, they can afford to be open with others. The promise is "having ascended all these degrees of humility we will arrive at that love of God, which being perfect, casts out fear" (RB 7:67). Having discovered who we are and having opened ourselves to life and having learned to be comfortable with it, we know that God is working in us. We know, most of all, that whatever happens we have nothing to fear. Life may be unclear, life may be difficult, but we are free of the false hopes and false faces and false needs that once held us down. We can fly now. Let all the others scratch and grapple for the plastic copy of life. We have found the real thing.

Humility is simply a basic awareness of my relationship to the world and my connectedness to all its circumstances. It is the acceptance of relationships with others, not only for who they are but also for who I am. I do not interact with others to get something out of it; I make my way with all the others in my life because each of them has something important to call out of me, to support in me, to bring to fruit a vision of God in my life.

Humility is not a false rejection of God's gifts. To exaggerate the gifts we have by denying them may be as close to narcissism as we can get in life. No, humility is the admission of God's gifts to me and the acknowledgment that I have been given them for others. Humility is the total continuing surrender to God's power in my life and in the lives of those around me.

The inner courtyard of our monastic community is seen by few but depended on by many for that glimpse of beauty we need in life to always see it anew. It seeps into our bones and our subconscious like the fine art of humility. It is there nourishing us quietly and calling us to something more worthy than the distractions of the day. It calls us to reality.

6

Monastic Mindfulness: A Blend of Harmony, Wholeness, Balance

They will regard all utensils and goods of the monastery as sacred vessels of the altar, aware that nothing is to be neglected. They should not be prone to greed, nor be wasteful and extravagant with the goods of the monastery, but should do everything with moderation and according to the abbot's orders.

RB 31:10–12

The stained-glass windows of our chapel are a riot of color. Because the chapel has an east-west orientation, we are flooded with gold light from the left side of the altar during morning praise and bathed in blue light during vespers in the early evening. Every window carries a different concept and a different design. Every window has its own meaning. And yet they come together somehow in my mind and soul. I do not easily remember them only one at a time. I think of the windows all at once, and all at once they tear at my soul and work on my unconscious and stretch all the senses in me as we sing, "Now that the daylight fills the sky, we lift our hearts to God on high." I never fail to be amazed at how all those colors and all those tiny pieces of glass and all those forms and figures go together without conflict. Then one day I realized that it was the light itself that gave all those different things integrity. It was simply light that blended them together and made them one for me.

I began to wonder what it was that gave all the other differences of life unity and integrity. What is it that makes for unity among the many opposing energies we meet in life that could instead become just so many instances of noisy clash and conflict? What is it that brings life together and people together and the world together and nature together? What is it, not in them, but in me that connects us all and makes harmony and wholeness possible in a fragmented life?

Then I remembered the line in the Rule: "Treat the tools of the monastery as if they were the vessels of the altar" (RB 31:10). Clearly, in Benedictine spirituality, everything is sacred and everything is one. The awls, the rakes, the trough, and the chalice. All treated in the same breath. The ancients understood the notion well.

One day a traveler begged the Teacher for a word of wisdom that would guide the rest of the journey.

The Teacher nodded affably and though it was the day of silence took a sheet of paper and wrote on it a single word, "Awareness."

"Awareness?" the traveler said, perplexed. "That's far too brief. Couldn't you expand on that a bit?"

So the Teacher took the paper back and wrote: "Awareness, awareness, awareness."

"But what do these words mean?" the traveler insisted.

Finally the Teacher reached for the paper and wrote, clearly and firmly, "Awareness, awareness, awareness means ... Awareness!"

Awareness of the sacred in life is what holds our world together and the lack of awareness and sacred care is what is tearing it apart. We have covered the earth with concrete and wonder why children have little respect for the land. We spill refuse into our rivers and wonder why boaters drop their paper plates and plastic bags and old rubber shoes overboard. We pump pollution into our skies and question the rising incidence of lung cancer. We produce items that do not decay and package things in containers that cannot be recycled. We fill our foods with preservatives that poison the human body and wonder why we're not as well as we used to be. We make earth and heaven one large refuse dump and wonder why whole species of animals are becoming extinct and forests have disappeared and the ozone shield is shriveling.

We're a people who lack awareness. We're a world that has lost a sense of balance. We're a people for whom wholeness is a frayed and sorry notion. The assembly-line culture has atomized our production process and our way of thinking as well. No one sees the consequences of their actions come together anymore as carpenters and builders did in the periods of history before us. It takes a real leap of insight now to go from the moral implications of welding missile canisters to the ethical possibility that we are colluding in the planned destruction of the globe. It's so hard to think that the herbicides I use in my garden contribute to the poisoning of the planet. Or that the emission from our third car is one emission too many for the neighborhood. Or that things, things, things are crowding out our senses and our souls. Or that time has gone crazily askew.

In the face of all of that, Benedictine spirituality does not ask the monastic to be a pauper or a stranger in the land. Monastics, the Rule declares, are to be given "the proper amount of food" (RB 39), "the proper amount of drink" (RB 40), "the clothing of the region, whatever they need" (RB 55:1–2). No, destitution is not of the essence of Benedictine spirituality. Benedictine spirituality asks simply for harmony, awareness, and balance. Benedictine spirituality asks us to spend our time well and to be careful that our wants are not confused with our needs and to treat the world and everything in it as sacred. Benedictine spirituality asks us to recognize our connectedness. Benedictine spirituality calls us to be mindful.

Benedictine spirituality asks us to be mindful about things. Monastics must learn to use what they are and what they have for the good of the human race. We have to learn to be mindful that creation belongs to God and we have only been put here as its keepers. Each of us has been given something to keep well: a small garden, a tiny room, a simple apartment, our bodies. That much, surely, we could take care of mindfully.

Two ideas militate against our consciously contributing to a better world. The idea that we can do everything or the conclusion that we can do nothing to make this globe a better place to live are both temptations of the most insidious form. One leads to arrogance; the other to despair. The fact is that we can, however, be mindful of our own worlds and so, perhaps, make others more mindful of theirs.

Somehow, monastic mindfulness recognizes that small actions are global in their scope and meaning. People who would not litter in a church will litter on the highway because they see no connection between the two. A monastic mentality, on the other hand, considers the two actions the same.

The monastic knows the world has become an inter-locking village—big, bureaucratic, impersonal, remote. Decisions made in one part of the world have long-range consequences for the rest of it. Pollution of the Great Lakes eventually affects the water systems of the whole earth. Destruction of the South American forest lands re-duces the air quality of the entire hemisphere. Concen-tration of mineral resources in the hands of a few retards the development of half the families of the world. The control and consumption of energy sources by some make technology unavailable to most. The weak are ig-nored. Women are excluded. The powerful are enslaved by their own devotion to profit rather than quality.

In the middle of all of this, though, the monastic lives in one monastery in one small place with a one-eyed, single-minded mindfulness of that piece of the Garden. In the midst of all this, Benedictine spirituality requires all of us to go through life taking back one inch of the planet at a time until the Garden of Eden grows green again. The fact is that where those who follow the Rule of Benedict live, the world will become an ordered, cared-for place. Resources, people, products, and time become precious.

Monastic mindfulness sees everything as one: the peo-ple of the earth, the resources of the earth, the products of the earth. Each of them is to be used in ways that do not injure any of the others. Each of them is to be cared for well. In a culture that depends on planned obsoles-cence, that builds things in ways that assure their break-down, monastic mindfulness comes to recall that one more desk discarded before its time is one more tree lost to the globe. The question is not, "Is another desk avail-able in our time?" The question is, is another desk nec-essary in our time? If not, what will replacing it mean for the populations of the future? Plastics and their pollutions? Plywood and its lack of beauty? Formica and the loss of the natural anywhere in life?

Benedictine spirituality is a spirituality of transformation. The land is to be transformed from the barren to the bountiful; life is to be transformed from the chaotic to the ordered; thinking is to be transformed from the scattered to the centered; relationships are to be transformed from the exploitative to the ennobling. Everything necessary is to be provided, yes, but the Rule says clearly: "the vice of private ownership" is to be "completely uprooted" (RB 33:1).

To do that, a lot of things have to change. We have to quit listening to the ads that are designed to seduce us. We have to pare life down to its simplest base. We have to come to understand that we have been allotted our portion of the goods of the earth; we have not been given the goods of the universe for our own personal consumption. We own this earth in common with the poor. We have to learn the difference between needs and wants so that the needs of all can be supplied, which doesn't mean that my own life must be narrow or restricted. It simply means that I must come to understand the difference between having it all and having everything.

I may need to get out on the lake at sunset to cleanse my soul and drain off the tensions of the day. But I do not need to go into debt to do it. A small boat will do, not the newest, not the best, not the largest motor. If it's the experience I want and not the exhilaration that comes from the envy of others, then a nice, safe, seaworthy little craft will provide me the spiritual experience of solitude and quiet and immediate contact with the God of nature without having to compete with the U.S. Navy in the process.

I may need to dress well for work and professional gatherings. But weekly shopping sprees and closets full of slightly worn silks are hardly necessary. A basic wardrobe and a few nice party things are surely enough in a world where the poor have nothing and the rich don't even remember what they do own.

I may need a car to get to work on time, but does it need to include every gadget known to modern marketing: four stereo speakers, two sheepskin seat covers, the brass-topped gearshift?

And most of all, do I have to have the top of the line in everything? Isn't it one thing to indulge myself in one aspect of life—my clothes, or my furniture, or my toys— and entirely another to do it in everything? The point is that once I begin to clutter my house with things that separate me from life, I have become unfree, a prisoner of consumption, a hoarder of artifacts. Then it's not exciting enough to just sit and look anymore, or walk and see anymore, or listen and respond anymore. I have to surround myself with things that are not real and do not fill the inside of me or of anyone else. They own me now; I don't own them.

Even when, years ago, the practice was for nuns to wear medieval garb, it was a Lenten practice in our community to do an annual inventory of goods and clothing. We wrote down "five coifs, three scapulars, three habits, seven books, one book bag" to determine where we were slipping over into accumulation. It was a chastening exercise that I have learned to miss. The question is, What would our lives look like on paper today? Simple and harmonious and whole, or silly and trivial and fiercely independent and depressingly insecure? The early monastics told of Abba Agathon, the desert master, who often went away to new places taking nothing with him but his knife for making the wicker baskets that were his living. But you and me? We accumulate all our lives and carry the things around with us until we have spent more time and money on things than we have on living.

Benedictine harmony and Benedictine balance demand a simpler approach to life, not for the sake of false asceticism but for the sake of human freedom. The gods we have made for ourselves take so much more adoration time than any human being has to give.

Benedictine harmony and balance require, too, a respect for time as well as for personal goods and planetary stewardship. The way we spend our time may well be our greatest resource and it will certainly influence what we do with the way we treat the earth we live on and the things we own.

Benedict was quite precise about it all. Time was to be spent in prayer, in sacred reading, in work, and in community participation. In other words, it was to be spent on listening to the Word, on study, on making life better for others, and on community building. It was public as well as private; it was private as well as public. It was balanced. No one thing consumed the monastic's life. No one thing got exaggerated out of all proportion to the other dimensions of life. No one thing absorbed the human spirit to the exclusion of every other. Life was made up of many facets and only together did they form a whole. Physical labor and mental prayer and social life and study and community concerns were all pieces of the puzzle of life. Life flowed through time, with time as its guardian. Not now.

With the invention of the light bulb, balance became a myth. Now human beings could extend the day and deny the night. Now human beings could break the natural rhythm of work and rest and sleep. Now human beings could begin to destroy the framework of life and turn it into one eternal day, with, ironically, no time for family, no time for reading, no time for prayer, no time for privacy, no time for silence, no time for time. Suddenly, we needed the wisdom of the Rule more than ever.

Somewhere in my formative years, I made the mistake of telling the prioress that the reason I wanted to be excused from Matins and the evening curfew was because I had a term paper to write for a college class which I had had no time to complete before that. She let her body sink back into her high-backed wooden chair from which point she could see me more piercingly, tapped her finger over her lips, and looked down at me over her glasses. "My dear child," she said slowly to make sure I didn't miss the import of the message, "we have all the time there is." The lesson got more meaningful as time went on. The fact is not that we don't have time for important things in life. The fact is that we don't take time for the important things in life. We don't take the prayer time. We don't take the reading and reflection time with Scripture. We don't take the time we need to make the family, family.

Our time gets totally out of balance. We spend it all on friends, or we spend none of it there. We spend it all on work, or we spend it all on our compulsions. We spend it all on the body, or we spend none of it on the body. We spend it all talking, or we spend none of it talking. We go from one personal prison to the next. And, eventually, there's no sense of monastic order—pray, read, work, serve, share, rest—at all. We wake up some day and realize we haven't heard from old friends for years; we haven't been to see our aging relatives in the local nursing homes for months; we don't know the names of our cousin's children anymore; we haven't fixed the family graves since the funerals; we haven't written a personal letter for years; we haven't sat in a large easy chair and read a good novel for ages; we haven't read a profound book since we got out of school. And life is flying by. All skewed.

Then, little by little, things in us go dry before we know they're gone. Church has become a mechanical function. Social life has become strained. A sense of achievement is gone. No one in the neighborhood knows who we are. Family life is dull. Our spiritual life has gone to straw. Living has become a numbing rather than an enlivening thing.

Balance, the Rule says. Balance. And harmony. And awareness. What I do not bring to life, life cannot possibly give me. Benedict says that we must bring a sense of order and awe and proportion and perspective. When the casinos stay open twenty-four hours a day and the TV movies show all night and noise seeps into every nook and cranny of life, it takes a special love of life to control it before it sweeps us away in a torrent of activities that clutter rather than cleanse us.

What are the signs of harmony and balance and awareness in our lives? People with a sense of Benedictine balance see that life is a medley of multiple dimensions, each of which must be developed. They have become more than either their work or their play. Nothing consumes them and everything taps something new in them. They walk through life smelling the flowers. They need enough money, some play, good work, steady friends, spiritual growth, intellectual stimulation, and harmony with nature. They do not set out to get all the money they can, to be invited to every party in town, to collect a prestigious circle of well-connected acquaintances, to make religion magic, or to become a body-building fanatic.

They make time for every facet of life. They live a rhythm of life that includes the natural, the spiritual, the social, the productive, the physical, and the personal. They can tell you each week what they have done in each area. They live life well. They are, in fact, fully alive.

To live a life of Benedictine harmony means we have to become caretakers of our world, not its enemies. We have to learn to love the natural again: natural grass and natural vegetables and natural air. We have to learn to care for what we have rather than casually destroy and unthinkingly replace things simply because they bore us. We have to learn to walk through life on tiptoe, not destroying, not trampling, not neglecting what has as much right to be here as we.

To live a life of Benedictine awareness means we must come to see what we cannot. To the monastic mind, everything speaks of God. What I have and what I do not have. What I want and what I do not want. What I care for and what I do not care for. But the message is not easily extracted. It takes reflection and prayer and the wisdom of others. Life takes working through. Life takes perspective. Life takes a sense of significance and a happy admission of insignificance. Life takes a willingness to deal with what we are and where we are and why. But I can't be rushing from meeting to meeting and paycheck to paycheck and party to party and store to store at breakneck

speed and expect to be able to do all of that. No, somehow or other, I have to begin to do it all consciously. With
more than now in mind, on the one hand, and with only
now in mind on the other.

Benedictine harmony and balance and awareness call
us all to life drunk deeply. And, interestingly enough, there
has probably never been a better moment in history to
do that. We have information that has never been known
before. We have a vision of the world and all of its people
and all of their needs that has never been known to humankind before this time. We have scientific insights that
are far beyond the understandings of our ancestors. We
have a level of technology that frees us to be humans, not
beasts of burden, that frees us to be thinkers on the planet
rather than mere survivors of its rigors. We have a mech-
anized life, a computerized life, and a connected life that
frees us and bonds us as at no other time in human history.

All we lack, now that life has become so speeded up,
is the will to slow it down so that we can live a little
while life goes by. We need to want to be human as well
as efficient; to be loving as well as informed; to be caring
as well as knowledgeable; to be happy as well as re-
spected.

It's not easy. But the Rule of Benedict says, "Take care
of everything, revere one another, eat and drink moder-
ately, pray where you work, think deeply about life every
day, read, sleep well, don't demand the best of everything,
pray daily, live as community" (RB 4). Be sure that one
part of your life is not warring against the other.

The light that penetrates all the separate windows in
the monastery chapel is what gives them balance and har-

mony. By themselves they are discordant and fragmented and competitive in their clamor for attention. My life is like that. All of its separate segments cry for my total attention. It is only the continued awareness that comes from the development of a perspective on life that is broader and deeper than any of them that convinces me that no one of them alone is worth it. Work can seduce us with our own godship. Too much play can make us shallow. People can become our chains. Even prayer can shrink our souls if prayer becomes an end unto itself, a chloroform rather than a consciousness.

Benedictine spirituality asks for so much more than that. Benedictine spirituality requires balance and harmony and awareness. Benedictine spirituality requires that we live life to the full.

7

Work: Participation
in Creation

They [monastics] must not become distressed if local conditions
or their poverty should force them to do the harvesting themselves. When they live by the labor of their hands, as our ancestors and the apostles did, then they are really monastics.

Those who are sick or weak should be given a type of work or
craft that will keep them busy without overwhelming them or
driving them away. The abbot must take their infirmities into
account.

RB 48:7–8; 24–25

We keep four things in our monastery that
I'm sure anyone else with a good sense
for order and efficiency would have thrown away long
years ago: an old spinning wheel, a vintage 1920 typewriter, an unused altar bread baker, and a shiny new
shovel with a bow around it. They sit out in plain view
for all the world to see in what we call "The Heritage
Room." There are no signs on them. No dates. No expla-
nations. They just sit there, reminding us, agitating us,
calling us.

The spinning wheel comes from the 1800s when the
nuns apparently made their own thread and cloth. I've

never seen it used, nor do I know anyone who has. The typewriter belonged to Mother Rose. She was one of the early intellectuals in the community and typewritten papers and community memos were her stock-in-trade.

The old altar bread iron I used myself as a young teacher in 1955. On Mondays I went to college and on Tuesdays I pleated the community headdresses. On Fridays I cleaned the community room, on Saturdays I did church work, and on Sundays I taught Sunday School. But on Wednesday afternoons I would rush home from teaching school, mix a runny batter, and bake communion hosts on that machine. I would bake until prayer time every Wednesday of every week.

The shovel we used in 1968 to break ground for the new monastery and we have never used it since.

Point: they're all old; they're all useless; they're all unused and they're all valueless. Why keep them?

I think I know. Silently, unceasingly, clearly, these artifacts of another age remind us that the work that brought us here must go on. They recall us to the truth that work is fundamental and necessary and physical and holy and spiritual and creative.

Work, you see, is a basic part of the monastic tradition. The Rule is full of it. There are no slaves in Benedict's monastery even in a period of slavery. There are no servants. "When they live by the labor of their hands, as our ancestors and the apostles did, then they are really monastics" (RB 48:8), Benedict says. We do not live off the labor of others. We are not to be a burden on society. We are not an elite. Those working in the fields at the hours of prayer are to stay in the fields and pray. Prayer is not to be used as an excuse not to bring the harvest in. Those about to begin a community service for the week are to ask a blessing on that work. Everyone is to serve at table. Everyone: the children of nobles as well as those who were the children of serfs.

Work in the monastic tradition is not something to be avoided. Work is not a punishment or a penance. Work is a privilege.

Among the earliest sayings of the Desert Monastics, one of the oldest stories passed from generation to generation, was a story about the purpose of work.

One day a holy monastic was going to town to sell some small articles in order to buy food to live on. A cripple on the roadside said, "Where are you going, Teacher?" And when the monastic said [he was going] to town, the cripple said, "Would you do me the favor of carrying me there with you?" So the Teacher carried the paralytic into the town.

Then the cripple said, "You can just put me down where you sell your wares." And the Teacher did so.

When the monastic sold an article, the cripple said, "What did you sell it for?" And when the monastic stated the price, the cripple said, "Will you buy me a cake with that?" And the Teacher did so.

When the selling time was over, the cripple said, "Now will you do me the favor of carrying me back to the place you found me?" And once more, the Teacher did so.

When they arrived at the place where the Teacher had found the paralyzed beggar, the cripple said, "You are filled with divine blessings, in heaven and on earth," and disappeared. Then the monastic realized that the cripple had really been an angel, sent to try both spirit and flesh.

Here, in this simple monastic story of the right of the wounded in society to make themselves part of our worlds and to profit from the fruit of our labors, all the modern-day attitudes toward work go awry. In the mon-

astic mind, work is not for profit. In the monastic mentality, work is for giving, not just for gaining. In monastic
spirituality, other people have a claim on what we do.
Work is not a private enterprise. Work is not to enable
me to get ahead; the purpose of work is to enable me to
get more human and to make my world more just.

The questions for contemporary society and the technological age are clear: Is non-work really an ideal? What
should we be doing when we are not working? And, how
is work in the monastic spirit different from work done
out of other perspectives?

There are two poles pulling at the modern concept
of work. One pole is workaholism; the other pole is pseu-
docontemplation.

The workaholic does not work to live. The workaholic
lives to work. The motives are often confusing and sometimes even misleading. Some workaholics give their entire
lives to work because they have learned in a pragmatic
culture that what they do is the only value they have.
Many workaholics don't work for work's sake at all; they
work for money and more money and more money. Other
workaholics work simply to avoid having to do anything
else in life. Work is the shield that protects them from
having to make conversation or spend time at home or
broaden their social skills. Sometimes, ironically enough,
work becomes the shield that enables people to get out
of other work. As a result, although the workaholic often
makes a very good contribution to society, it is often only
at the expense of their fuller, wiser selves.

Pseudocontemplatives, on the other hand, see work as
an obstacle to human development. They want to spend
their hours lounging or drifting or gazing or "processing."

They work only to sustain themselves and even then as little as possible. Pseudocontemplatives say they are seeking God in mystery, but as a matter of fact they are actually missing the presence of God in the things that give meaning to life. The biggest shock of my early life in the community was to find out that novices were not permitted to go to chapel between the regular times for prayer. Were not permitted. Now what kind of a place was this? Here I was, set to get instant holiness and impress the novice mistress at the same time, but someone apparently had figured out both motives and moved to block the whole idea. In fact, they had something much better in mind for all of us. They wanted us to work. Why?

Genesis is very clear on the subject. "Then God took Adam," Scripture says, "and put him in the garden to cultivate and to care for it" (Gen 2:15). Adam was put in the garden to till it and to keep it, not to contemplate it; not to live off of it; not to lounge. Even in an ideal world, it seems, God expected us to participate in the co-creation of the world.

The early Christians, including Paul, worked to sustain themselves. "You know that these hands of mine have served both my needs and those of my companions. I have always pointed out to you that it is by such hard work that you must help the weak" (Acts 20:34–35). And the Rule is equally clear: "When they live by the works of their hands, as our fathers and the apostles did before us, then are they really monks" (RB 48:8). The Desert Monastics, too, always worked. They braided baskets for sale to support themselves and to provide something of use to others, of course, but also to avoid what the ancients called *acedia*, a kind of lethargy that made the continued efforts of the spiritual life too much for the soul that was undisciplined and unexercised.

None of the great religious figures withdrew from reality intent on rapture alone. The rapture came from making reality better. And work was the key to it all.

Work is a Christian duty. Paul's rule was "Those who would not work should not eat" (2 Thess. 3:6–12). And Benedict's rule was "Idleness is the enemy of the soul. Therefore, the monastic should have specified periods for manual labor as well as for prayerful reading.... Even the weak and delicate should be given some work or craft" (RB 48:24).

Now those are crucial concepts. In one swift phrase, work and meditation are put on the same level in Benedict's rule. Work is not a nuisance to be avoided. Work is a gift to be given. Clearly, holiness and work are not mutually exclusive ideas. Work, on the contrary, is a necessary part of holiness in Benedictine life.

Surprisingly enough, in a document on the spiritual life, Benedict treats work first after prayer and at more length than *lectio*, the meditative reading of Scripture. There is to be no doubt about it: the monastic life is not an escape from responsibility nor is it membership in the local country club. The Benedictine is to be about tilling and keeping the garden of life in the most serious of ways.

Western culture has not treated work kindly. We have a history of serfs who worked like slaves and sweatshops that robbed people of their human dignity and basic rights. We have lived in a capitalism that bred brutal competition and unequal distribution of goods as well as inventiveness and profit. We are watching the poor get poorer even while they are working. We see the rich get richer even when they don't. And we realize that the middle class must work harder every year just to stay where they were last year. What can possibly be good about all of that? That depends on the work we do and why we're doing it.

In Benedictine spirituality, work is what we do to continue what God wanted done. Work is co-creative. Keeping a home that is beautiful and ordered and nourishing and artistic is co-creative. Working in a machine shop that makes gears for tractors is co-creative. Working in an office that processes loan applications for people who are themselves trying to make life more humane is co-creative. Working on a science project, on the other hand, whose sole intent is to destroy life makes a mockery of creation. To say that science is blind, that science is objective, that science is neutral when what you make is napalm and the components of germ warfare and plutonium trigger-fingers is to raise ethical questions of overwhelming proportions. Here Benedictine spirituality confronts the casuistry and clever moral gyrations of this time with the sign of the accusing presence of Christ. Benedictine work is intent on building the Kingdom, not on destroying it.

In Benedictine spirituality, work is purposeful and perfecting and valuable. It is not a time-filler or a money-maker or a necessary evil. We work because the world is unfinished and it is ours to develop. We work with a vision in mind. After the person with a Benedictine soul has been there, the world ought to be a little closer to the way the Kingdom will look.

Work is a commitment to God's service. The parable of the unproductive fig tree is a dramatic one. The fruit tree that does not do what it can do and should do, Jesus curses. To have a gift that can nourish the community and to let it go to waste strikes at the very heart of community. I must be all that I can be or I can't possibly be anything to anyone else. God the creator goes on creating through us. Consequently, a life spent serving God must be a life spent giving to others what we have been given. To refuse to do for the other what we are more than capable of doing simply because we do not like to do it, is to deny the very reason for which we are who and what we are.

The man who is a good cook but refuses to cook because "cooking is woman's work" while his wife struggles to do the wash and take care of the children and keep the house clean and handle her own job at the same time is not serving God with the gifts he has been given. Young people who are too busy with their own agendas to help around the house but have no problem eating there are not serving God. The woman who won't spend extra time on the office job or admit that she can transcribe as well as translate manuscripts when both services are sorely needed is not serving God with the gifts she has been given. People who won't admit their talents for fear they'll be asked to use them are not simply being selfish, they are refusing to serve God.

Laziness and irresponsibility are forms of injustice and thievery. They take from the people of the earth. We were not put on earth to be cared for. We were put on earth to care for it.

But that is hardly the message we get in a world intent on making the greatest amount of money with the least amount of effort. That is certainly not the message we get in a world where money talks. In a Benedictine community we are never permitted to link the money we earn with the things we need. We aren't given the use of a car because we earn a salary large enough to support one. We are given the use of a car because we need it, for whatever, whether we earn a salary or not. Spending time with shut-ins, serving soup in soup kitchens, visiting our families, getting to our ministries are all exercises in gift giving that may or may not earn salaries. The point is that Benedictine spirituality demands we give what we have to give simply because it is needed and because we have it to give, not because it will fill our pockets. Work, in other words, is to be done for its own sake, not because we feel like it or because doing it will necessarily enable us to garner some profit for ourselves. No, work is a great deal more important than that.

Work develops the worker. The fact of the matter is that work is the one exercise in gift giving that always comes back to the giver. The more I work at anything the better I get at it. And the better I get at something, the better I feel about myself. It is the fear of being good for nothing that destroys people, but skill in anything develops only with practice and practice and practice. Everyone knows the difference between a good teacher and a poor teacher, a good manager and a poor manager, a good telephone operator and a poor operator, a good porter and a poor one, a good gardener and a poor one. And they all got that way by working, with concentration, with commitment and, often, with long hours. With the transformation of the forty-eight-hour week into the forty-hour week and now the slow but clear move to the thirty-hour-week or part-time employment, the whole notion of work for pay will have to change. Some work will be done to live, of course, but some work will have to begin to be done simply because work has something to do with being alive and being left with a garden to "till and keep."

In the Benedictine tradition, labor is dignified and so are the laborers. In a society where work was a sign of lower status in society, where nobles never expected to work a day in their lives, where slavery was considered a natural state in life, everyone worked in Benedict's community. "The members should serve one another," the Rule mandates. "Consequently, no one will be excused from kitchen service unless they are sick or engaged in some important business of the monastery, for such service increases reward and fosters love" (RB 35). Humility is something to be demonstrated, not talked about. Service is its own reward. Love comes from loving. Ironically, it is what I have cared for that I grow to care about. Work and community, it seems, are inextricably linked. People who tell you they love you but never do a thing for you, people who say they value the family but never join the family in any project, people who say they care about the planet but never do a thing to make the planet a more human place to live, fail to see that life is an exercise in co-creation. And that requires work.

Work is essential, then, both to community development and to justice. But the justice works both ways. Benedictine spirituality not only requires that the worker do justice to the community, but that the community do justice to the worker. Give them the help they need, the Rule says (RB 53). Give them enough to eat (RB 39). Let them get enough sleep (RB 8). Listen if they say the job is too hard for them (RB 48).

The life questions with which the Rule of Benedict confronts our age become, consequently: What do I expect of the people who work for me? Can they live decently on what I pay them? Do I allow them a life of their own? What are my real expectations of them—a forty-hour-week or response to my nod and call? Are they people in my life or only pieces of another kind of machinery? Do I even know the names of the typists in the pool? It is so easy to become elitist, even in a classless society. All we have to do is to make people invisible. But Benedictine spirituality simply defies that kind of life. We're told to honor one another, whoever they are.

Work makes time worthwhile. There is a romantic notion that monastics spend time gazing into space. Well, not with my novice mistress you didn't. She understood best the admonition of the Rule, "Work while you have the light of day" (RB 41:8), and she strained to teach it to us, for our sakes and for the sake of the world around us. Sloth, she taught us, was not a monastic virtue.

Time, we learned through regularity and responsibility, is the treasure that cannot be recovered and must not be taken for granted. Time is all we have to make our lives bright-colored, warm, and rich. Time spent on an artificial high is time doomed to failure. Time spent amassing what I cannot possibly use and which will not change my measure of myself even if I do use it, is time wasted. Time spent in gray, dry aimlessness is a prison of the thickest walls. But good work that leaves the world softer and fuller and better than ever before is the stuff of which human satisfaction and spiritual value are made. There will come a moment in life when we will have to ask ourselves what we spent our lives on and how life in general was better as a result of it. On that day we will know the sanctifying value of work.

Work has been one thing that our culture has done best. Every American child is encouraged to get a paying job from the age of six. We have been trained to be responsible and productive. As a result, the Western world fast became the industrial center of the world where a few people could out-farm, out-produce, and out-organize every other area of the world. But we have some serious by-products of the Puritan notion that hard work is a claim on God's blessings and a sign of God's favor as well. Success and efficiency and opportunity and elitism and alienation have marked us too. The drive for success at work, instead of success in life, continues to make people ill and to destroy marriages and to increase the level of personal dissatisfaction.

Efficiency has become a god that will accept the sacrifice of people for the sake of the production line. The days of hand-carved chairs from an artist's hands have given way to plastic molds for the sake of profit though it's clear that we need beauty and community in this world today more than we need one more product of anything. We need to learn that there are some things worth doing in life that are worth doing poorly, if doing them perfectly means we will have destroyed people for the sake of producing the product. Do we need paper clips in this world? Absolutely. Do we need to make them faster and distribute them more broadly than anyone else in the world in order to make more money than anyone else in the paper clip business? Not if it means that we must drive the workers who make them beyond their endurance and ourselves beyond the humane to do it.

Opportunity has made dilettantes of us all. We run through the candy store of life always looking for the better job and the better pay and the better office. Nothing is ever good enough in the quest for success. Instead of settling down, we work constantly with one eye on the next office, the next opening, the next promotion. Instead of being who we are where we are, we are always on our way to somewhere else in this culture. So making friends with the neighbors is not a high priority. After all, we won't be here long. Keeping the word that sold the product is of little consequence. We won't be here when the customer complains. Developing a conscience about what we do and how we do it is hardly important. By the time it fails or is uncovered we will have been long gone. And our family lives and human development will have been long gone with it.

The disassociation that comes from being only one small point on the assembly line of modern life has dulled our consciences and blinded our eyes to our own part in a world where death is our greatest export. The days are gone when the family that tilled the field also planted and harvested it together. Now owners own and planters plant and sprayers spray and pickers pick and sellers sell and none of them takes responsibility for the pesticides that reach our tables. Scientists calculate and designers design and welders weld and punchers punch and assemblers assemble and none of them takes responsibility for a nuclear world.

The implications of a Benedictine spirituality of work in a world such as this are clear, it seems:

- Work is my gift to the world. It is my social fruitfulness. It ties me to my neighbor and binds me to the future. It lights up that spark in me that is most like the God of Genesis. I tidy the garden and plant the garden and distribute the goods of the garden and know that it is good.

- Work is the way I am saved from total self-centeredness. It gives me a reason to exist that is larger than myself. It makes me part of possibility. It gives me hope.
- Work gives me a place in salvation. It helps redeem the world from sin. It enables creation to go on creating. It brings us all one step closer to what the Kingdom is meant to be.
- Work, in the Benedictine vision, is meant to build community. When we work for others, we give ourselves, and we can give alms as well. We never work, in other words, for our own good alone.
- Work leads to self-fulfillment. It uses the gifts and talents we know we have and it calls on gifts in us of which we are unaware. It makes us open to new dimensions of our own personalities and talents as yet undiscovered.
- Work is its own asceticism. A Benedictine spirituality doesn't set out to create hair shirts or debilitating fasts as a pledge of commitment or a badge of spiritual discipline. No, Benedictine spirituality simply faces the work at hand, with all its difficulties and all its rigors and all its repetition and all its irritations—and accepts it. What today's work brings is what is really due from me to God.
- Work, finally, is the basic Benedictine way of living poverty and being in solidarity with the poor. The Benedictine doesn't set out to live off of others. The Benedictine doesn't sponge and doesn't shirk and doesn't cheat. Benedictine spirituality gives a day's work for a day's pay. Sloughing work off on those

down the pecking order from us, assuming that personal days are automatically just additional vacation days, taking thirty-minute coffee breaks in the fifteen-minute schedule, doing one coat of paint where we promised to do two, is not a Benedictine way of looking at work in the Garden.

Like the monastic who meets the beggar on the way to market, the purpose of work in Benedictine life is to carry others, to care for them, and to see them safely home. The old spinning wheel and typewriter and altar bread baker and shovel in our Heritage Room are clear proof of how well that has been done by those before us. The task of a corporate society whose guiding star is the bottom line and whose measure of value is money must somehow do the same.

8

Holy Leisure:
The Key to a Good Life

We believe that the times for both [prayerful reading and manual labor] may be arranged as follows: From Easter to the first of October, they will spend their mornings after Prime till about the fourth hour at whatever work needs to be done. From the fourth hour until the time of Sext, they will devote themselves to reading.

Above all, one or two seniors must surely be deputed to make the rounds of the monastery while the members are reading. Their duty is to see that no one is so apathetic as to waste time or engage in idle talk to the neglect of the reading.... On Sunday all are to be engaged in reading except those who have been assigned various duties.

RB 48:2–4; 17–18; 22

Nothing in the monastery fascinates me as much as our use of candles and vigil lights. You would think that in a world of fluorescent lights and rheostats, gooseneck lamps and incandescent bulbs that candles and lamp stands and vigil lights would be long gone. But no, not here. Not in my monastery. We hang them burning in the monastery hall outside of chapel during Holy Week and we light a candle for thirty days after the death of a sister and we give them as a sign of perpetual profession and we carry them when we renew our baptismal promises. Candles and vigil lights focus our minds on the light of Christ and remind us always of the ebb of our lives. They tell us that day is slipping by. They tell us that it is time to look into the dark spots of our souls and bring light there. They teach us not to burn the candle at both ends.

And, as time goes by in the Benedictine life, if you contemplate a candle long enough, you come to understand the Rule and get the message. It has been part of this community forever, I think.

Years ago, before the lakefront erosion washed it down the shale bluff on which it sat, a gazebo perched on the outer edge of the shoreline that fronts our monastery. Even on Ninth Street, the site of the original monastery in the center of town, a small cloister yard was set aside for walking. Now there are trails that go deep into our woods behind the monastery and a small sunset deck on every cabin on the property. Every night I watch the sisters leave the house to walk along the creek that winds its way through our property to the lake. In early autumn and spring the dining room patio and residence hall porches are full of quiet people. In the wintertime, a fire crackles downstairs nightly while the snow beats against three walls of windows. Everywhere we look, in other words, there is the call to come apart and rest awhile that has been part of the community soul for years. These are busy people, these sisters of mine. They work with the poor and console the dying and feed the hungry and witness to peace and care for the elderly and teach the underprivileged and study and serve and welcome and give warmth everywhere they are, day after day after day. But they are never too busy, it seems, to realize that life is not only lived in doing. They are not so involved in work that they forget that we have no light to give to others unless we first of all have it in ourselves.

The most rigorous ascetics of all, the early Desert Monastics, considered the problem as well, it seems. Was all of life to be a penance? Was all of life to be hard work? Was all of life designed to exhaust the body in order to save the soul? Was all of life meant to be spent pouring oneself out? In answer, they began to tell a story about Abba Anthony.

One day a hunter in the desert saw Abba Anthony enjoying himself with the brethren and he was shocked. What kind of spiritual guide was this?

But the old monk said to him, "Put an arrow in your bow and shoot it." So the hunter did. Then the old man said, "Now shoot another." And the hunter did. Then the elder said, "Shoot your bow again. Keep shooting; keep shooting; keep shooting." And the hunter finally said, "But if I bend my bow so much I will break it."

Then Abba Anthony said to him, "It is just the same with the work of God. If we stretch ourselves beyond measure, we will break. Sometimes it is necessary to meet other needs." When the hunter heard these words he was struck with remorse and, greatly edified by Anthony, he went away. As for the monastics there, they went home strengthened.

Leisure, in other words, is an essential part of Benedictine spirituality. It is not laziness and it is not selfishness. It has something to do with the depth and breadth, length and quality of life.

In an American culture, however, leisure may also be one of the most difficult spiritual elements to achieve. We are trained to be doers and makers, not dreamers and seers. Benedictine spirituality, on the other hand, sets out to develop people who reflect on what they are doing, people for whom the gospel is the filter through which they see their world.

Work, it is clear from the Rule of Benedict, must not exist in a vacuum. Monastics do not exist to work. Work is to be integrated into monastic life without doing violence to either. In the Benedictine vision of life, no one dimension of life is to be exclusive. Prayer, community, and personal development are all as essential to the good life as work. And that takes a sense of holy leisure.

Scholars of the Talmud say that the Sabbath is emphasized in Genesis not to show that God needed rest, because that would be heresy, but to show that God created rest and that God demanded rest. Rest, Sabbath, the rabbis insisted, were essential to creation for three reasons.

First, they argued, the Sabbath equalized the rich and the poor. For one day a week, at least, everyone was the same. On the Sabbath, the rich could not oppress the poor or control the poor or consume the poor. On the Sabbath, rich and poor were equally free. Second, the rabbis taught, the purpose of the Sabbath was to give us time to evaluate our work as God had evaluated the work of creation to see if our work, too, was "good." Finally, the rabbis declared, the purpose of the Sabbath was to give us time to contemplate the meaning of life.

In fact, the rabbis pointed out, if one-seventh of every week is rest, then one-seventh of life is rest: 52 days a year, 3,640 days in seventy years—or ten years of sabbath, rest, and reflection in a lifetime, which are all designed to be used for reflection on meaning. Sabbath, in other words, is that period for holy leisure when I take time to look at life in fresh, new ways.

In his plan of life, Benedict set aside four hours a day

for prayer, six to nine hours a day for work, seven to nine hours for sleep, about three hours for eating and rest, and three hours a day for reading and reflection time. I remember the kind of surprise that came over me when, after years in the community, I suddenly realized one morning in chapel at the daily oral reading of the Rule that Benedict wasn't saying that someone should be sent around the monastery to see if people were doing their work. He was saying that they should be sent around the monastery to see if the monastics were doing their reading and reflecting (RB 48). The community should be mindful, in other words, to see that people were taking time to live a thoughtful as well as a productive life.

Benedict's schedule, of course, is an agrarian and monastic one. It does not work for families with small children. It does not work for people who commute across large cities. It does not work for those whose workday runs from early office hours to evening appointments. But if Benedict's hours don't compute for us, his ideas are more important than ever. We may not be able to keep that particular schedule, you and I, but we must find a life rhythm that somehow satisfies each of those elements.

The question for a time of rapid transit and conference calls and triple-shift work days is balance. And the answer is balance too.

But what is balance in a society whose skewing of time has it totally off balance? What is balance in a culture that has destroyed the night with perpetual light and keeps equipment going twenty-four hours a day because it is more costly to turn machines on and off than it is to pay people to run them at strange and difficult hours? In the first place, balance for us is obviously not a mathematical division of the day. For most of us, our days simply do not divide that easily. In the second place, balance for us is clearly not equivalence. Because I have done forty hours of work this week does not mean that I will get forty hours of prayer and leisure. What it does mean, however, is that somehow I must make time for both. I must make time, or die inside.

Leisure has two dimensions, play and rest. The Benedictine Rule does not talk about play because play was built right into sixth century life by the church calendar. One of the functions of holy days and festivals, most of which started in churches and religious communities, was to provide both the privileged and the peasants of the society with space and time for common enjoyment. On Church feasts commoners could not be required to work. Play was the Church's gift to the working class in a day before labor unions and industrialization.

Now, in this century, we even have to learn how to play. Indeed we have more opportunities for play than generations before us, but we have managed to make most of our play simply a special kind of work. We organize our ball teams into leagues and our running into races and our swimming into exercise programs and our tennis into tournaments. The movies are violent and the plays are expensive. It costs money to take children to the zoo to see animals that once could be seen in the backyard for nothing. Toys must be educational and of infinite variety. Play has become big business in the United States, and so most of America has taken to television watching instead to avoid their anxieties and their exhaustion, with the Fourth of July and the Memorial Day weekend the only recognized deviations from the anesthetizing social norm.

The notion of celebrating life as communities and families together, the underlying value of the old church feasts, is long gone. The balance of family and social recreation is becoming harder and harder to come by. The balance of work and real play, activities done for no purpose at all except the release and recapture of energy, is becoming foreign. As a consequence our souls are drying up in work and our minds are being numbed by TV nothingness. We need to learn to play again if our spiritual lives are going to be healthy at all.

But play is not the only indicator of non-work or personal growth, and it is not at all the dimension that Benedict treated. The leisure that Benedictine spirituality deals with is holy leisure, leisure that is for holy things, leisure that makes the human more human by engaging the heart and broadening the vision and deepening the insight and stretching the soul. Benedictine spirituality is more intent on developing thinking people than it is on developing pious people. It is one thing to pray prayers; it is another thing to be prayerful.

To understand leisure is to avoid being one of the lemmings of life who follow the crowd and follow the boss and follow the party line. Holy leisure asks, What is it to follow the gospel in this situation, now, here? Holy leisure means I take time to step back and ask what's going on in this, in them, in me. I take time to try to understand what the Jesus-life demands in this situation.

Our scholastic director told us repeatedly, "No matter how valuable your work, remember that the empty vessel must be filled." The message was clear. You can't give anybody anything unless you have something inside you to give. Machines can do the computation and animals can do the heavy work. Only you can bring spiritual quality to wherever you are, but first you must have it yourself. And it must be nourished, regularly.

Holy leisure, in other words, is the foundation of contemplation. There is an idea abroad in the land that contemplation is the province of those who live in cloistered communities and that it is out of reach to the rest of us who bear the noonday heat in the midst of the maddening crowd. But if that's the case, then Jesus who was followed by people and surrounded by people and immersed in people was not a contemplative. And Francis of Assisi was not a contemplative. And Teresa of Avila was not a contemplative. And Catherine of Siena was not a contemplative. And Thomas Merton was not a contemplative. And Mahatma Gandhi was not a contemplative. Obviously, some of our greatest contemplatives have been our most active and most effective people. No, contemplation is not withdrawal from the human race.

The problem is that we must learn to distinguish between purpose and meaning in life. Purpose is part of what it means to be white, Western, American. Purpose has something to do with being productive and setting goals and knowing what needs to be done and doing it. It is easy to have purpose. To write seven letters today, to wax that floor, to finish this legal brief, to make out those reports, to complete this degree, that's purpose. Meaning, on the other hand, depends on my asking myself who will care and who will profit and who will be touched and who will be forgotten or hurt or affected by my doing those things. Purpose determines what I will do with this part of my life. Meaning demands to know why I'm doing it and with what global results.

Contemplation, therefore, is not a vacation from life.

Contemplation is the pursuit of meaning. The contemplative is intent on determining the relative value of things in life. The contemplative believes that everything we do either advances or obstructs our search for meaning in life. Those who find the will of God everywhere and feel the presence of God anywhere are the real contemplatives.

Real contemplatives don't separate political morality and private morality. They know that all of life is one. Real contemplatives don't think in terms of this world and the next. They know that life is simply an ongoing process, only part of which is clear to us at any one time. Real contemplatives don't substitute daydreaming for doing the will of God. In the midst of the greatest spiritual moments in the record of humankind, Moses was sent away from the burning bush, Joseph was sent to take care of Mary, Mary Magdalene was sent to tell the apostles of the resurrection. The moment of enlightenment, it seems, comes not for itself but for the sake of the mission. Immersion in the God-life demands a response, not a rest. Real contemplatives don't spend life staring into space. That kind of contemplation can simply become a disguise for pure escape, or worse, for selfishness. Idleness is not a synonym for contemplation.

Real contemplation, in other words, is not for its own sake. It doesn't take us out of reality. On the contrary, it puts us in touch with the world around us by giving us the distance we need to see where we are more clearly. To contemplate the gospel and not respond to the wounded in our own world cannot be contemplation at all. That is prayer used as an excuse for not being Christian. That is spiritual dissipation.

Contemplation is the ability to see the world around

us as God sees it. Contemplation is a sacred mindfulness of my holy obligation to care for the world I live in. Contemplation is awareness of God within me and in the people around me. Contemplation is consciousness of the real fullness of life. Contemplatives don't let one issue in life consume all their nervous energy or their hope. God is bigger than this problem at work or this irritating neighbor at home or this dependent relative in the family. God is calling me on and on and on, beyond all these partial things, to the goodness of the whole of life and my responsibility to it.

That's enlightenment. When I myself am the total square footage of my own small world, that's darkness. When my pains and my successes and my agendas are my only concern, that's darkness. When I see no larger meaning in my life than my own interests, that's darkness. But when I begin to look at life through the eyes of God, then enlightenment has finally come.

But enlightenment and contemplation, the relationship between the goals of my life and the meaning of my life, take more than wishing. Inner vision and direction can only come from keeping my heart centered on God and my mind open. That's where Benedictine spirituality is balm and blessing in a world gone wild with activity for its own sake.

Dom Cuthbert Butler made the point that it is not the presence of activity that destroys the contemplative life but the absence of contemplation. The genius of Benedictinism is its concentration on living the active life contemplatively. Benedictine spirituality brings depth and focus to dailiness. Benedictine spirituality is as concerned with the way a thing is done as it is with what is done:

guests are to be received as Christ (RB 53); foods are to be selected with care (RB 39); the goods of the monastery are to be treated reverently (RB 32); pilgrims and the poor are to be treated with special attention (RB 66)—and all for the love of Christ. Life is not divided into parts holy and mundane in the Rule of Benedict. All of life is sacred. All of life is holy. All of life is to be held in anointed hands.

And so Benedict calls all of us to mindfulness. No life is to be so busy that there is no time to take stock of it. No day is to be so full of business that the gospel dare not intrude. No schedule is to be so tight that there is no room for reflection on whether what is being done is worth doing at all. No work should be so all-consuming that nothing else can ever get in: not my husband, not my wife, not my hobbies, not my friends, not nature, not reading, not prayer. How shall we ever put on the mind of Christ if we never take time to determine what the mind of Christ was then and is now, for me.

So, contemplation does not take non-work; contemplation takes holy leisure. Contemplation takes discipline.

In the period before the renewal of religious life that was mandated by Vatican II, every minute of the monastic day was directed by the superior and minutely ordered. We prayed and meditated from 6:00 A.M. until 7:30 and then ate and went to school. At 5:00 P.M. we went to prayer and reading again. At 7:30 we said night prayer, had two hours for study, and went to bed. Since Vatican II, the times for community prayer are still there but the reading periods are expected to be done privately. We were all sure, given the multiple individual schedules in a community of many ministries, that this was the preferable way to go. And I still think it was. But now it is clear that contemplation is something we have to work very hard at attaining.

At the end of a long day, it is so much easier to curl up with the newspaper or slump in front of the TV than it is to wrestle with the Scriptures. At the beginning of a busy day, it is so much more tempting to get an early start on what won't get finished anyway than it is to stay in chapel and let the Word of God seep slowly in as a guide to the day's reality. We all tell ourselves that things are just too hectic, that what we really need is play, not holy leisure. We all say we'll do better tomorrow and then do not. We all say the schedule is too crowded and the children are too noisy and the exhaustion is too deep. But, if we do nothing to change it, the schedule just gets worse and the noise gets more unrelenting and the fatigue goes deeper into the bone. The fact is that it is our souls, not our bodies, that are tired. That fact is that we are so overstimulated and so underenergized that the same old things stay simply the same old things, always. The sense of excitement that comes with newness and freshness is gone. Only contemplation, the recognition of meaning in life, can possibly bring that kind of energy back. But that means we have to make time for ourselves for holy reading and gentle awareness and deep reflection. How else can we come to understand what relationship really means in life? How else can we hope to make sense out of the senseless? How else can we come to control what has control of us, if not by putting things in perspective and putting self in perspective and putting the God-life in perspective.

So, contemplation takes time and contemplation takes discipline. Contemplation also takes depth. In contemplation we stretch our understanding so that our hearts can come to peace. Contemplation is not emptiness that ends in fullness. Contemplation is fullness that ends in emptiness. I can't become a contemplative by sitting and waiting. I must become a contemplative by listening and waiting.

The monastery candles tell me day after day: time is going by, the light is waning, there are some kinds of uselessness that are essential. Then I have to make a choice. What is time for? If time is only for work, then what will be left of me when the work is gone? If there is no light in me, what will happen when darkness comes, as darkness will, to every life? What is the gain of leading a useful life if I do not also lead a meaningful one?

Abba Anthony knew what this culture must relearn: play and holy leisure are the things that make work possible, that make work worthwhile.

9

Giftedness:
Making Music Together

Monastics will read and sing, not according to rank, but according to their ability to benefit their hearers.

If there are artisans in the monastery, they are to practice their craft with all humility, but only with the abbot's permission. . . . Whatever products of these artisans are sold, those responsible for the sale must not dare practice any fraud.

RB 38:12; 57:1; 4

There are those who would consider it a strange collection of musical instruments for a monastic liturgy. There is an organ, of course, but the major difference between the liturgical music we have now and liturgical music as we knew it years ago is that the organ is not the only instrument on which we depend for Eucharistic services. On the contrary. There's a set of handbells and a pack of guitars and a grand piano and a harpsichord and a hammered dulcimer and a flute and a trumpet and a recorder and a bass guitar and a harp and a xylophone and dozens of finger bells. And they're all played by different sisters. I love the music that comes from all those variations, but more than that I love what the grouping itself says about the place of the person in community.

Some of those musicians are professionally trained. Some of them are amateur instrumentalists from their earliest years. Some of them know little or no music at all. All of them love what they're doing. And all of them are doing it for the sake of the community as well as for their own pleasure. All of them are using their gifts together in praise of God. All of them respect one another's talents, none of them expects to be the whole show, and each of them knows that without the other her own contribution will fail. But, when each of them does what she can do with the best possible spirit and the best possible preparation, then the entire community liturgy is deeper and more beautiful for all of us than it could possibly be without her. In fact, the whole community is stronger because its individuals have brought their very special strength to it.

The art of community life in general lies in the balance of the person and the group. Benedictine spirituality exacts two things: self-giving and self-development; family order and family understanding. Any one of these without the others reveals a person or a group gone askew.

Individuals do not exist for groups. That is fascism. That is the philosophy that makes it possible to shoot football players full of steroids so the team can win and then abandon the players when the steroids don't work on their broken bodies any longer. That is the philosophy that makes young men cannon fodder for the fatherland. That is the philosophy that turns people into interchangeable parts for the company. That is the kind of parenting that leaves young people unhappy for years as they try to live out the aspirations of their mothers or the expectations of their fathers.

Groups exist for people. The function of a group is to enable people to achieve together what they cannot possibly achieve alone. Groups are meant to make our highest personal hopes achievable through common search and common effort and common discipline. Groups, communities, and families provide the environment in which individuals can become what they most seek to be.

So, in a Rule written for community life, Benedict has a great deal to say, at least implicitly, about the individual. And the cornerstone of this psychology of life in Benedictine spirituality is that every individual is different. And must be treated differently. And must be seen differently. And must be developed differently.

The Desert Monastics knew the truth of human uniqueness, which they relate in this story about Abba Arsenius:

Once when Abba Arsenius was ill he was taken by the brothers to a church and put on a bed with a small pillow under his head, an unheard of comfort for monks of that time. Now, behold, a monk who was coming to see him for spiritual guidance, saw him lying on a bed with a little pillow under his head and he was shocked. "Is this really Abba Arsenius, this man lying down like this?"

Then, one of the monastics took the visiting monk aside and said to him, "In the village where you lived, what was your trade?" he asked.

"I was a shepherd," the visitor replied.

"And how did you live then?" the monk continued.

"I had a very hard life," the visitor answered.

Then the monk said, "And how do you live in your cell now?"

And the visitor said, "Oh, now I am very comfortable."

Then the monk said to him, "Do you see Abba Arsenius? Before he became a monk he was the father of the emperor. While you were in the world as a shepherd you did not enjoy even the comforts you have now but he no longer leads the delicate life he lived in the world. So you are comforted always, while he is afflicted always."

The visitor prostrated himself saying, "Father, forgive me, for I have sinned. Truly the way this man follows is the way of truth, for it leads to humility while mine leads to comfort." And the monk withdrew, edified.

The monastic lesson is clear: every one of us has a special set of needs and differences, and we must accept those in one another and attend to them. That is the basis of a communal spirituality. "Let those who have need of more," the Rule reads, "ask for it humbly. And let those who have need of less thank God" (RB 34).

The person is to be cherished. Benedictine spirituality is not an attempt to reduce every human being to a least common denominator. It's not about turning individuals into homogenized groups. Benedictine spirituality is about bringing the uniqueness in us and around us to holiness. Now, no doubt about it, it is not easy to decide when cherishing the person is to be preferred to maintaining the good order of the group. When should one member of the family get privileges that the others do not get? When should one person's needs be allowed to eclipse the equally important needs of others?

Benedict posits some important principles. Do not start by expecting everyone to be alike. Benedict, for instance, requires two kinds of vegetables at every meal so that people can have choices (RB 39). Everyone is to have a bed of their own, which was no small thing in sixth century Europe (RB 22). And everyone is to have clothing suitable for the place (RB 55). The monastics are even encouraged to ask to be relieved of the work they've been given to do if they feel that it's beyond them (RB 68). Life is not a one-size-fits-all affair. The notion of leading life without wishes and without interests in the name of spiritual development may indeed be a worthy type of asceticism, but it is clearly not Benedictine asceticism.

Everyone gets whatever it is that they need to live, in other words, and everyone gets to contribute to the decisions that have been made about their lives. There is no sense of artificial asceticism here, no made-up penances, no militarism in the style of community governance. Just life lived raw. The purpose is not to make life hard for others on the grounds that difficulty will be good for them. Life is hard enough as it is. The purpose is simply to live the normally hard parts of life together and well.

Most important is the place of personal weakness in Benedictine spirituality. This is only "a little Rule," Benedict wrote. "For beginners." And nothing "harsh or burdensome" is prescribed (RB 73). This is a rule for you and me, in other words. You and I know ourselves to be beginners in the spiritual life, no matter how intense our efforts or how sincere our search or how long our years. And you and I don't want anything that looks too complex. And you and I are not the kind who go around looking for the harsh or burdensome. On the contrary. You and I are Americans and Americans aren't even allowed to have a headache.

The truth of Benedict's awareness of the fragility of the likes of us is nowhere clearer than it is in the chapter on the qualities of the abbot (RB 2:64). What Benedict says the abbot must be is a sure reflection of what Benedict knew that each of us would be.

In the first place, Benedict says that the spiritual leader of the community should be elected by the community itself. Obviously Benedict believes that we are sincere in our individual search for direction in the spiritual life and that we are capable of finding it. He knows, though, that we need to become deeper, more centered people, and that putting forth the effort to get it is half the process. The spiritual life is not something that is given to us; it is something we must learn to seek with all our hearts. The choices that we make in our leaders is a measure of our own character and commitment to growth. If the latest rock star is our leader, it will show. If the local money makers are our leaders, it will show. If the civil religion is where we get our values and ideals, it will soon show. Benedictine spirituality requires us to take responsibility for the leadership we choose and to choose carefully.

Second, the abbot must be chosen for wisdom, not age. But, if that's the case, then you and I must be looking for wisdom, not for identification with the latest fad of the youth cult or the security of the cautious and conservative elderly. It's neither the new Church nor the old Church that will save us—in other words, not the right wing or the left wing of anything. It is wisdom alone, those insights into the truth of life that are distilled from the gospel and personal experience, that we must look to for guidance, not the latest in spiritual gimmicks or psychological schools or easy-come, easy-go gurus. Benedict knows what we need is wisdom, but too often we let ourselves settle for less. We want quick fixes instead of the slow and steady truth of life well lived.

Third, the abbot is told to serve the monastery, not to rule it. But if it is service we're to look for, not magic answers or blind direction, then each of us must learn to cooperate rather than simply to obey. It's so easy to take orders but to resist taking responsibility. If I'm told to do a thing, I do it. But if it is not my night to do the dishes, they stand in the sink. If it is not my job to mop up the kitchen floor, it stays sticky. If it is not my responsibility to speak to the people in the waiting room, they stand there unattended at the counter. I do my part and not a single thing more. It's so easy to give our service but not our hearts.

It must be mutuality that we bring to life, not control and not convenience. A snap of the fingers is not what life is about. A happy home is not a home where he gives the orders and she and the children jump. A good family is not one where she lays down the law and everybody else tiptoes around. A good family is not one where the children become the total criteria of the schedule and the activities. A good family is one where we all serve one another and where everyone's needs count.

Life is about learning to grow through the growth of others. The people that we live with and work with have something to give to our spiritual development. We have to learn to take the raw materials of our lives and turn them into the stuff of sanctity. We can't wait for the perfect person or the perfect environment to call us to spiritual maturity. The people in our lives are the people who will test our virtues, our values, and our depth. Benedict knew that the call to serve rather than to dominate would mean that people had to learn to cooperate with others rather than to depend on them. The problem is that either domination or dependence demands so much less of us than collaboration.

Fourth, the abbot must be more intent on mercy than on judgment. But if that is the case, then clearly Benedict knew that the world was made up of the very imperfect, the very human where a great deal of mercy would be necessary as we each wound our stumbling, human way to God. We, on the other hand, find it so hard not to expect perfection of ourselves and, because of that, to expect it of others as well. We drive ourselves and drive everyone around us beyond any achievable standard and then wonder why we fail and fail and fail. Benedictine spirituality says that life is a set of weaknesses in search of wholeness and we must be patient with one another's growth.

Finally, the abbot must be open to counsel. The meaning is clear: everyone has a wisdom, an insight, a concern, a truth, a gift. And everyone of us is capable of giving it. In our weaknesses we are still valuable, still capable of being unselfish and objective, still worthy to be heard.

The concepts that emerge from this treatment of the person are entirely different from those we have come to know in modern culture. In Benedictine spirituality, no one ever stops being worthwhile . Not in any occupation. Not at any age. In Benedictine spirituality, people are seen as individuals, not as members of the team or members of the army or members of the class. Each of them has particular needs and each of them has particular gifts and each of them has particular responsibilities too. And though none of them are called to be what they are not, each is also called to be everything she can be. It's a lesson our society dearly needs to relearn.

We have learned a great deal about the "Self" since Freud, but we may not have learned nearly so much about the "We." Instead, parents are blamed for the problems of adult children. Teachers are blamed for the drift away from universal literacy in this country. Police departments are blamed for the rising incidence of crime. Poverty is blamed for personal decadence. The concept of sin has given way to the notion of development. It's surely time to ask when and where individual responsibility for the common good will again begin to play a part in personal life.

There is no doubt that this generation comes from a period that had managed to confuse the moral, the immoral, and the amoral beyond much recognition of any of them. Murder, missing church, and swearing, all occupied the same moral category. Puritanism and Jansenism, historic theories of the basic and essential evil of human nature, had done their work so well that when studies in personal development began to emerge in the 1950s, they found an audience eager to have their wrongdoings absolved and bent on proving that their present problems were a result of past circumstances, not accountable to them. People from alcoholic families blamed their homes for their present sense of rootlessness. People from broken homes blamed their parents' problems for their own feelings of alienation from others. Children from poor homes blamed their poverty for their lack of discipline.

Benedictine spirituality offers a different model, harsh

sounding in this day perhaps, but nevertheless more dignified in its assessment of the person than many more modern ideas. Benedict calls for correction, and even for punishment, if "having been told, the monastic does not amend" (RB 28:1). The point is we are, most of us, capable of change. We are not puppets at the end of a sociological string. Booker T. Washington emerged from the peanut fields of the country. Caesar Chavez came out of the barrio. Jesse Jackson was an illegitimate child. Most of us have had something to overcome—alcoholism in the family, major illnesses, financial need. The Rule of Benedict simply assumes that good will is enough to make the difference. The Rule of Benedict does not assume that everyone can do the same things equally well—"Let only those read who can edify" (RB 38:12), the Rule directs— but he does assume that everyone can and must do something for the rest of the community. Everyone can and must help to carry everyone else. That's what community, that's what family is all about. Alone we may be little but together we can be something.

So the Rule of Benedict calls everyone to work at something the community needs and calls everyone to work for holiness and calls everyone to serve and calls everyone to help make community decisions. There is no room here, in other words, for family members who expect to be picked up after simply because they earn a salary. There is no room here for the frail to shift all the dishes onto others simply because they are subject to chronic headaches. There is no room here for forgiveness from life. There is no room here for me to absent myself from responsibility for the human race.

That, I believe, is the purpose of the Benedictine vow of stability. The vow of stability is not intended to attach a person to a place. Stability is intended to attach a person to a group, as family does, as nation does, as ethnicity does. The vow of stability says life is an enterprise to be undertaken together, not an entertainment to be indulged in alone. I'm not responsible for someone else only when I feel like it or when it's not too much trouble. I'm responsible always, everyday, for all these people to whom I am continually related until one by one we have helped one another all the way through life.

In a culture where the family meal is a practice almost extinct, where family chores are done for money, where every member of the family has a schedule independent of all the others, where the elderly either live alone or in nursing homes, responsibility to the family as a whole is a value to be sought after and a prize to be achieved. But, without it—as Benedict implies in his choice of the community model over the eremitical tradition—each of us will simply be another rolling stone. We'll touch group after group in life, perhaps, but the question, is will they ever touch us? Who will ever know us well enough to dare to confront our idiosyncrasies? Whom will we ever know well enough to have our need for control and our gift of compassion tested and tried? In what way will we make the contribution to life that every person is born to make?

Responsibility is as much a part of personhood, in other words, as uniqueness. The same Rule that made provision for what everybody else of that period said a monastic didn't need or shouldn't have—good food, adequate drink, decent clothes, weakness and mercy and help—is also the spiritual document that told the buyer of the monastery to be patient with people and the community not to ask for things "out of time" (RB 31). Benedict wanted the servers to eat before the community meals so they wouldn't find the task too much for them but exacted, too, that all the monastics would serve one another (RB 35). He allowed the artists and craftspeople in the monastery to practice their special gifts but warned them never to overcharge the buyers (RB 57). He wanted the abbot to have a prior with whom to share the burdens of administration but told the prior quite clearly that his role was to follow the abbot's goals, not to devise a separate set that would confuse or divide the community (RB 65). He said that the sick were to be cared for, but he also wrote a chapter of the Rule to the sick themselves, telling them not to be demanding (RB 36). Uniqueness and independence are clearly not synonyms in the mind of Benedict of Nursia. Uniqueness and responsibility go hand in hand in Benedictine spirituality. By all means I should be who I am and have what I need, but you have a claim on those gifts. Those gifts were given to me as much for your sake as for my own. The community does not exist to make me possible. Together we exist to make the gospel possible.

We're in a period in society today when people work together for years and never come to know one another; when we know more about what is happening in Bangladesh than we know about what is happening in the next block; when families are scattered across the country and even the world; when people live in apartment complexes for years and never say hello to their daily companions in the building elevator. In a social climate like that, it is so easy to have our worlds shrink to the size of our own desks and our own houses and our own agendas. We call it individualism, but the fact is that it is really self-centeredness. "No one is to pursue what they judge better for themselves, but instead, what they judge better for someone else" (RB 72:7). Each of us has the responsibility in Benedictine spirituality to take care of the others as well as to take care of ourselves.

There is no question that my goal in life must be to develop the best in myself to the best of my ability. The question is, Why? In Benedicitine spirituality, the answer seems to be that we grow to full stature in life in order to carry someone else. Perhaps, in fact, we never grow to full stature until we have learned to carry someone else. That's the value of uniqueness and that's the meaning of responsibility. That's why spoiling children is such a sad gift to give the child. How else, if not in their homes, will they ever learn that their lives are not for themselves alone?

That's what the visiting monk learned at the bedside of Abba Arsenius and that's what the musicians teach us every Sunday morning as they use multiple instruments, sophisticated and simple, together and alone to bring us all to fullness of life.

10

Hospitality: The Unboundaried Heart

All guests who present themselves are to be welcomed as Christ, for he himself will say: "I was a stranger and you welcomed me" (Matt. 25:35).

Once a guest has been announced, the superior and the community are to meet the guest with all the courtesy of love. First of all, they are to pray together and thus be united in peace....

Great care and concern are to be shown in receiving poor people and pilgrims, because in them more particularly Christ is received; our very awe of the rich guarantees them special respect.

RB 53:1; 3–4; 15

Lots of things have changed since I entered this monastery. We used to wear medieval clothes and now we use contemporary dress. We used to be silent at meals and now we talk. We used to pray in Latin and now we pray in English. We used to engage in only one ministry, teaching, and now we try to contribute to the upbuilding of the Kingdom in multiple ways. I have learned to expect things to change in every area and most things have. With one notable exception. From the first day I entered this community up to this very morning, we have had our own fresh baked bread.

I used to wonder about that. After all, you can buy bread just as cheaply as you can bake it these days. And to see anyone put all of that effort into such a thankless task seemed sometimes to be a pity. Every day, the flour is mixed in large, heavy, metal mixing bowls and the dough is patted into single loaves for baking and dropped into baking tins and rubbed by hand with butter and shoved into the heavy ovens. Despite all the work and time and physical effort it took to prepare it all, the bread is long gone by evening, day after day, year after year. What is there to show for all that work?

Then, to make matters worse it seemed, with commercial companies all over the country offering to perform the service of packaging and sorting wafers for us, the community chose instead to make its own Eucharistic bread every day as well. Now this is a busy community, with multiple responsibilities and heavy work loads and crowded schedules. Why would anyone add one more thing to days that are already overfull, especially since the task could just as well be done by someone else, anyone else?

Finally, with money low and little to spare ourselves, the community discovered that the city around us in this declining industrial area was full of hungry men and anemic women and undernourished children—the homeless, the unemployed, the working poor. And, one by one, we opened a soup kitchen and a food pantry and a food bank. Once a year now, the sisters empty their rooms of all the clothes and things they don't need and send those to the food pantry, too, to be given with the food bags so that joy and beauty and a sense of care accompany the staples.

Some people call it foolish. We can't possibly feed everyone who is hungry. The few things we have to give—a picture here, a blouse there, a knickknack perhaps, a small tape recorder maybe—won't fill anyone's home or add much to their barren lives. They are essentially useless things in a hopeless situation. It all seems to be an impossible venture. And where will the money and gifts come from to keep it up?

Then, someplace along the line I came upon one of the sayings of the Desert Monastics that explained the situation:

One day someone handed round a few dried figs to the monastics in the community. Because they were not worth anything, no one took any to Abba Arsenius in order not to offend him. Learning of it, the old man did not come that day to the community gathering, saying, "You have cast me out by not giving me a share of the blessing which God has given you and which, apparently, I was not worthy to receive." Everyone who heard of this was edified. Then, one of the monastics took him the small, shriveled up, dried out figs and Arsenius came to the community synaxis [prayer] again with joy.

I discovered, you see, that real Benedictinism requires us to pour ourselves out for the other, to give ourselves away, to provide the staples of life, both material and spiritual, for one another. The question is not whether what we have to give is sufficient for the situation or not. The question is simply whether or not we have anything to give. That's what hospitality is all about. Not abundance and not totality. Just sharing. Real sharing.

Hospitality has become very organized and very antiseptic in the United States today. We take into our lives only the friends we've made on the job, or the neighbors we know, or strangers that someone else can vouch for, but not the unknown other or the social outcast or the politically unacceptable foreigner. We don't simply bake bread and pass it around freely: to the old black woman who cleans the halls, or the stranger who just moved in next door, or the young welfare mother who brings her food stamps to shop in the same supermarket we do. We have to be much more careful than that in a society where people are not safe in their own homes or welcome in their own neighborhoods or secure in the subways of their own cities. So, is hospitality an impossible art for this time and this culture?

To the people of the ancient Middle East whose lives were literally a desert, hospitality was a survival mechanism. Like boaters who never ignore the needs of another boater because there is no telling on the high seas when they themselves will need help, the people of the desert—glad for company that brought psychological nourishment and aware of their own possible peril of being in a place someday with high sun and no water—opened their tents and begged strangers to come in. The Scriptures are full of examples of hospitality: Abraham and Sarah open their tent to passing strangers; the Samaritan cares for the wounded on the side of the road; Lot shows greater commitment to the guest than to his own family.

The Rule of Benedict—written at a time of great social migration and personal peril, long before there were campgrounds or large motels—charged the monastery to "receive guests as Christ" and to take special care of "the poor and of pilgrims." "Guests," Benedict wrote, "are never wanting in the monastery" (RB 53). The monastery, in other words, was to be no bastion against the outside world. On the contrary, the monastery was to be a place of comfort and of solace and of safety for everyone. The monastery was the place where anyone would be welcomed, where rich and poor alike could come and find seats side by side despite the world around them where status counted dearly and classism was a given.

Benedictine spirituality says that we must continue to beg the stranger to come into our lives because in the stranger may come the only honesty and insight we can get in our plastic worlds. The abbot is instructed to listen to the criticism of the stranger because, the Rule teaches the community, "God may have sent that one for that very reason" (RB 61). The problem is that we may need to learn to practice hospitality of a different kind these days to get the same results.

In our world it is easy to let the Holiday Inns and the City Missions carry the burden of caring for strangers and absorbing the flow of life that teems at the gates outside of our offices and stands along the far fringes of our backyards and our neighborhoods and our churches, quietly present but barely seen and seldom noticed. Benedictine spirituality says that to become whole ourselves we must learn to let the other in, if for no other reason than to stretch our own vision, to take responsibility for the world by giving to it out of our own abundance, to make the world safe by guarding its peoples ourselves.

The world, it seems, has never been more in need of hospitality. Refugees roam the world displaced for political reasons by leaders who live in marble houses, while the soldiers they deploy die in ditches and the people they terrorize run from country to country seeking peace and safety for their children and human dignity for themselves. Tent cities are being built in the United States of America for the unemployed homeless of the richest nation in the world. Children flock to the cities in droves, out of abusive homes and divided homes and poor homes and good homes that simply can't handle them. The elderly are abandoned in old houses with leaking roofs and dirty windows and uncut yards. Foreigners are named enemy simply because they are foreign, apparently, and do not think or live or look like we do.

And who cares? And who does anything about it? Indeed, hospitality is the missing value of the twentieth century. Churches that promote the Sanctuary movement are prosecuted. People who employ undocumented aliens trying to clothe and feed themselves by good, honest work are fined and jailed. Yet the masses of the world are surging across our television screens and across our borders looking for hope but burdened with despair because hospitality is now defined simply as graciousness in high places and the affluent reception of the affluent.

The question is, Why? And the answer is that the biblical value of hospitality has been domesticated and is now seen more as one of the social graces than as a spiritual act and a holy event.

Like the monastics under Abba Arsenius we do not share our figs with everyone anymore, either because we have decided that the things we have are too good for the poor who need them or too simple for the rich who don't.

We have to learn how to take people in again or the poverty and the political hatred and the decimation of peoples and the turning of our own lives into icy islands will never end. We must learn in this century again to open our minds and open our hearts and open our lives and open our talents and open our hands to others. That is the hospitality for which the Rule of Benedict calls.

Benedict called always for an open mind. That's why Scripture reading is such an important part of Benedictine life. The fact is that Jesus was an assault on every closed mind in Israel. To those who thought that illness was a punishment for sin, Jesus called for openness. To those who considered tax collectors incapable of salvation, Jesus called for openness. To those who believed that the Messiah had to be a military figure, Jesus was a call to openness. It is impossible, in other words, to become immersed in the Benedictine spirituality of *lectio*, the deep and reflective reading of the Scriptures, and not be called to the hospitality of the mind that makes room for the AIDS patient or the politburo member or the notion of nuclear disarmament. Until we make room in our minds for the ideas of the gospel, there will be no way to get anything through the barriers of our own fears or prejudices into our lives.

Benedict is very specific about hospitality of the heart. The "bruised reed" is never to be broken. The knocker at the gate is always to be met "with all the gentleness that comes from the fear of God" and "provided a prompt answer with the warmth of love" (RB 66). Honor, courtesy, and love are the hallmarks Benedict requires for hospitality of the heart (RB 52).

It is so easy to give clothes to the poor but refuse to honor the ones to whom we have given the goods. Who says "Pardon me" to the down-and-outers who hang at the kitchen doors and garbage cans of our cities? Who sits and talks to the unskilled workers who clean the office buildings of our towns? Who makes friends with the people on the other side of town, the ones who aren't "our kind of folk?"

Everyone—everyone—is received as Christ. Everyone

receives a warm answer—on the phone, at the door, in the office. Sarcasm has no room here. Put-downs have no room here. One-upmanship has no room here. Classism has no room here. The Benedictine heart is to be a place without boundaries, a place where the truth of the oneness of all things shatters all barriers, a point where all the differences of the world meet and melt, where Jew and Gentile, slave and free, woman and man all come together as equals.

But whatever happens to the heart is the beginning of revolution. When I let strange people and strange ideas into my heart, I am beginning to shape a new world. Hospitality of the heart could change American domestic policies. Hospitality of the heart could change American foreign policy. Hospitality of the heart could make my world a world of potential friends rather than a world of probable enemies.

Yet, Benedictine hospitality is more than simply thinking new thoughts or feeling new feelings about people we either thought harshly of before or, more likely, failed to think about at all. Benedictine hospitality demands that we open our lives to others as well. Benedictine hospitality demands the extra effort, the extra time, the extra care that stretches beyond and above the order of the day.

Opening our lives to others is another dimension of Benedictine hospitality for our times. When Benedict wrote the Rule, the local village was the center of every person's universe. To this day, there are small mountaintop villages in Italy that are basically untouched by the outside world. No one goes into them much and no one leaves them. But today it does not matter if you and I ever leave our villages or not. Today the world comes, unbidden but persistent, to us. Television has become our window to the world. Newspapers and magazines, our eyes. We know that the poor are poor and that the elderly are lonely and that the children are hungry. We know that the politicians are declaring wars and that younger generations are dying in them. We know it's happening. We don't often know why.

And that's where we fail in hospitality. We are not opening our own lives to the plight of those around us. We don't understand the situations and we don't care.

Real hospitality for our time requires that, instead of flipping the channel or turning the page, we try to determine what it is about our own lives that is affecting these others. We have to wonder how we can help the poor at the doorstep who live thousands of miles away. Hospitality says that the problem is mine, not someone else's. It is my door and my heart upon which these people are knocking for attention.

In some places of this world, drought is destroying food supplies for years to come. But every time we use spray cans that emit the substances that burn holes in the ozone layer we ourselves contribute to the drought. It is not that the poor of the world are suffering. It is that the poor of the world who are crying out for help are of our making. The garbage that the world can't dispose of is made up of the Styrofoam cups we use and the tin cans we've discarded rather than recycled. It is what we spray on our gardens and inject into our animals that is ruining the national health.

Real hospitality for our time requires that we consider how to take these concerns into our own lives so that others can live a safe life too.

When guests came to Benedict's monastery, they were

fed and given lodging and cared for like one of the family. That took time and effort. That was hospitality of the open hand. It is not enough simply to change our minds about things or to come to feel compassion for something that had never touched us before or even to change our own way of life to let in the concerns of others. Real hospitality lies in bending some efforts to change things, to make a haven for the helpless, to be voice for the voiceless. We have to learn to take our own sense of home to others. What I do not want for my own family and friends, I do not want for others; what I would do for them, I will do for others:

- If I would not serve poisoned food to those I love, then I will write postcards to our legislators asking them to see that others are not poisoned by the food production process either.
- I will volunteer at the food bank or soup kitchen once a month to see that others are fed.
- I will join a group that is interested in ecology.
- I will send money I earned the hard way to groups that need support if the world is to get to be a better place for all of us.
- I will, in other words, do something.

I cannot go on thinking that nodding to neighbors in the parking lot is hospitality. I cannot fool myself into thinking that being nice to those who are my kind and my class suffices for the moral dimensions of hospitality.

Hospitality means we take people into the space that is our lives and our minds and our hearts and our work and our efforts. Hospitality is the way we come out of ourselves. It is the first step toward dismantling the barriers of the world. Hospitality is the way we turn a prejudiced world around, one heart at a time.

There will be racism in the world until you and I begin to take the other races in. There will be prejudice, until you and I take the other groups in. There will be war, until you and I begin to take the enemy in. There will be classism, until you and I begin to take the other segments of society into our own worlds and lives and parties and neighborhoods.

The Rule of Benedict is a tonic for human separations. Benedict takes in the poor and the pilgrim, the young and the old, the rich and the deprived, the ones of our own family of faith and the passersby. And every guest is received with the same warmth and the same care, the same dignity and the same attention.

The Rule of Benedict is also sensible about it. The monastics of the place are told to greet the guests but not to linger in talking to them. We all have our own lives to live, our own obligations to meet, our own schedules to run. Hospitality is not an excuse for lack of organization or purpose in our own circumstances. No, hospitality is the willingness to be interrupted and inconvenienced so that others can get on with their lives as well.

The clerks who ignore people at store counters, the teachers who ignore the parents of the children they teach, the wealthy who never even see the doorman or the cabdriver or the cook, the powerful who never hear the powerless, the religious ministers who are too busy to minister, are all examples of a world deprived of the spirit of hospitality.

Once you understand all of that, you understand without being told why the monastery bakes fresh bread daily and why the Eucharistic host is done in our own kitchen and why we opened a soup kitchen and a food bank and a food pantry and why we have a community giveaway once a year. Hospitality doesn't exist unless we go out of ourselves for someone else at least once a day. There is no hospitality where I can't think a new thought and see a new perspective and talk to a new person and give part of myself away day after day after day. Hospitality is one of those things that has to be constantly practiced or it won't be there for the rare occasion. The breads are the lifelong symbols of that, the perpetual reminders, the constant measure of a hospitality that is trying to be real at every level and always.

The disciples left Abba Arsenius out of the distribution of figs because they had forgotten that hospitality is the act of giving what you have to everyone in sight. It is not a series of grand gestures at controlled times. It is not a finishing-school activity. It is an act of the recklessly generous heart.

II

Obedience:
Holy Responsibility

It is love that impels them to pursue everlasting life; therefore, they are eager to take the narrow road of which Jesus says: "Narrow is the road that leads to life" (Matt. 7:14). They no longer live by their own judgment, giving in to their whims and appetites; rather they walk according to another's decisions and directions, choosing to live in monasteries. . . .

This very obedience, however, will be acceptable to God and agreeable to others only if compliance with what is commanded is not cringing or sluggish or half-hearted, but free from any grumbling or any reaction of unwillingness. For the obedience shown to superiors is given to God.

RB 5:10–15

The vow ceremony in our community is an awesome one. The sister about to make vows stands up in the midst of the community gathered in chapel and announces her intention to join it forever. When the prioress calls her, she brings her vow paper to the altar step where the prioress is standing, reads her vow profession aloud, and then carries the document to the place on the altar where together the newly professed sister and the prioress sign and seal it. Finally, the two walk back around the altar. But this time, it is the prioress who carries the vow document and places it on the altar while the new monastic sings three times in alternation with the community, "Uphold me, O God, and I shall live and do not fail me in my hope."

It's a very moving and a very symbolic event. It says that a person has freely and independently chosen to put herself at the disposal of a group and "under a Rule and a prioress" for the sake of the gospel. A woman comes to the altar alone but leaves it as part of a community. A woman makes a decision to put herself in the hands of someone who will now become part of all the major decisions of the rest of her life. In other words, a woman stands up in public and says, "I am not an entity unto myself." And then, suddenly, she is stronger for it and the gospel is safer for it too.

It's a far cry from rugged individualism. The questions are: Is it normal? Is it healthy? Is it natural? Is it good? After all, what happens to personal development when individuals give away the full control of his or her own lives?

The answer, of course, is that no one really has full control of their own lives. We're all limited by something. The difference is that some people decide what they will allow to control them and some people simply find themselves controlled by the whims and fancies of life. All of us meet and wrestle with authority. The only question is to what authority have I surrendered and how do I myself use authority when I have it. Authority and self-determination are two of the major problems of the spiritual life. Are we our own masters or not?

The Benedictine answer is a simple one. Benedictine communities cannot be pictured correctly by either the pyramid or the circle. Benedictine communities are not meant to be either hierarchical or egalitarian. On the contrary. Benedictine communities are better pictured as a wheel with a hub and spokes. In the Benedictine community, there is a center to which all the members relate while they all relate to one another.

The role of authority in Benedictine spirituality is to unify the community and to direct its attention to God who is the center of life of each and all of them. Benedictine authority is not for its own sake. Obedience for the sake of obedience can be sheer domination. Benedictine authority is not militaristic. The role of authority in the Benedictine community is not to make wives and children and monastics jump through spiritual hoops in order to prove their willingness to jump. No, Benedictine authority is designed to call us to our best selves by calling us, not to a system, but to the gospel. Monastics of another time and place demonstrated the difference well:

Once upon a time a visitor came to the monastery looking for the purpose and meaning of life.

The Teacher said to the visitor, "If what you seek is Truth, there is one thing you must have above all else."

"I know," the visitor said. "To find Truth I must have an overwhelming passion for it."

"No," the Teacher said. "In order to find Truth, you must have an unremitting readiness to admit you may be wrong."

The story is a clear paradigm of Benedictine life. The fact is that the person centered in Christ lives in a system in order to transcend the system. It is the ability to think thoughts other than our own, other than the past, other than the safe, other than the acceptable that will lead us eventually to truth. But to do that we have to learn to deal with our need to control. We have to learn not to be authoritarian with one another. We have to learn to discipline our constant urges to license. We have to learn, in other words, to listen to others and hear their truth.

Community, the story implies, depends on our ability to let things be what they are so that by learning from the struggles and frustrations of the day, we can all gain the fullness of life of which we are capable. What we need to learn is that everything will not always be to our liking in life, but if we can learn to let people do what they need to do, life will be good nevertheless. We lose the chance to find truth when we give the other either too much or too little control over our lives. When we become totally dependent on the ideas and directions of another in a blind and unexamined way or when we set out to dominate the lives of others ourselves, that is when our authority problems really begin.

When I live only for the sake of an authority figure, that is dependence. Real truth does not come from swallowing even holiness whole. That is, at best, spiritual childishness. Real truth comes from following the directions of another because my own heart and mind and soul know that no matter what effort this demands of me, it requires more integrity and ends in more good than my own lesser way can ever gain.

When I live only to resist authority, that is license. Truth does not come from sheer resistance. To be against something just to be against it, even if I am right, is not truth. It is only self gone wild with a crippling kind of isolation that will eventually make me deaf to whatever is best for me in life. When I do not have a clearly better way, then another's way will not only do, it will develop me beyond the level of my own limited lights.

When I live only to wield authority over others, that is not insight and leadership; that is domination. Truth can never come without sharing authority with other members of the community. The truth that I suppress in others will limit my own growth.

None of those attitudes toward authority—dependence, license or domination—are healthy from a Benedictine point of view. The first negative view of authority, dependence, is simply a way to avoid responsibility and look holy at the same time. When I need the approval of others to justify every step of my life; when I lay on others the burden of my own decisions; when I need someone else's permission to do what I feel should be done; when I need someone else's direction to do what I know must be done, that's not obedience, that's immaturity. Or it's manipulation. Or it's very, very sad.

The Rule of Benedict does not call for dependence. Monastics are to "listen with the ear of the heart" and then "labor" to do what is required of them (RB Prologue). Obedience, in other words, lies in listening and in laboring and in knowing what is required of us. The manager, for instance, who can't make a decision without first checking to see if everyone agrees and everyone approves and everyone is sure it will work is not necessarily being obedient to the group. One of the functions of leadership is to lead, and weak managers may simply check and check and check with others because they are not capable of leading when it is required of them to lead. Benedict says that in matters of importance the abbot or prioress is to ask everyone in the community, "starting with the youngest," and then the abbot or prioress is to "do what seems best" (RB 3).

The asking, it is clear, is not for the sake of dependence; the asking is for insight and information. The responsibility remains.

When social approval is such a priority in my life that stepping to a different drummer is beyond me, dependence becomes a weight around my neck. The crowd never questions nuclear weapons; how can I? The group laughs loudest at ethnic jokes, so mustn't I? The crowd buys the latest and the best; shouldn't I? In instances like these, it must be internal authority that counts or I will be battered by wind after wind of social change and social pressure. Who I am and what I stand for will never be clear and never be witness. I will simply be at the mercy of other people's principles.

Dependence is not a social nicety that fits me for company or proves my neighborliness. It is an obstacle to psychological growth. The dependent person becomes the other instead of him or herself. Dependence is not a virtue. It is a substitute for character. To say, "My husband won't allow me to . . ." may be to fail as a wife, if for no other reason than it may signal my failure to become a fully adult person. There is a world of difference between "We talked it over and decided that I wouldn't . . ." and "I asked but he won't let me." On the public level, likewise, "My country, right or wrong . . ." is not patriotism. It is abdication of the responsibilities of citizenship. It allows politicians to make decisions about the welfare of this generation and of generations to come without the benefit of my experience and concerns. It says, let someone else be blamed.

Responsibility is obedience in the best sense of the word. Servility is obedience in the worst sense of the word. One is interdependence; the other is dependence. When the Teacher says, "To find Truth you must have an unremitting readiness to admit you may be wrong," he means that fullness of life depends on keeping our hearts open to finding God, again and again, not on fashioning for ourselves an eternal right way and then clinging to it. Benedict warns, "There are ways which some call right that in the end plunge into the depths of hell" (RB 7). The obedience Benedict wants is not dependence. It is obedience to the will of God and to the Spirit at work in all of us.

The second negative view of authority, license, is, however, a skewed notion of independence. License says that I am accountable only to myself. But that is not only sinful, it is absurd. When I drive a car, I am not responsible simply for myself, I am responsible for every other driver on the road. When I cook, I have the moral obligation to be concerned for everyone who will eat what I prepare. When I work on an assembly line, everybody else's work depends on mine. The whole world, in other words, is an organic whole, a system of interlocking parts meant both to hold me up and to stretch me at the same time. License is an attempt to sabotage the system, to be my own small world, to be my own measure of meaning in life.

Monastic spirituality is an antidote to license. In the monastic community, everybody exists for the other. The porter is to receive the guest with warmth and peace always (RB 66). Nothing is to be done without the permission of the abbot (RB 5). The Rule is preeminent (RB 1). Everyone, even the sick and the fragile, are to receive a community assignment, to make their contribution to the good of the whole (RB 35). The definition of authority in the monastic mind, then, is accountability and responsibility. A good many marriages, a good many businesses, a good many families, a good many nations could use this same definition.

One of the Western world's most serious problems is the tension between the group and the individual. Our culture trains people in individualism and then condemns them to live forever in groups, large groups. The Rule of Benedict, however, trains people to live in community. The question is, Why? Isn't the eremitical life the life of complete perfection and total dedication to God? And the answer is, yes it is, for some people. But not for most, and then only after they have learned the virtues that come from life in community (RB 1). Most social beings, however, are meant to find their sanctification by living under the authority of society. It is the community that forms community values and virtues in me. It is the community that provides the arena for mutual support. It is from the community that I get an example of life lived well. It is in the community that teaching becomes real. It is in the community that authority is meant to become a gift rather than an instrument of oppression. It is only in the community that I really learn to listen to the voice of God in one another and to see the face of God in the other as well as in my own. It is only in community that I can learn to wield patience as well as power. It is only in community that I can learn to obey the command to serve one another.

The Rule is quite clear about it all. Benedict writes, "This message of mine is for you, then, if you are ready to give up your own will, once and for all, and armed with the strong and noble weapons of obedience to do battle for the true King, Christ the Lord" (RB Prologue). Monastic spirituality is not principally for the sake of personal salvation or contemplative withdrawal. Monastic spirituality is meant to bring the reign of Christ to the world around us through a life of community consciousness of the will of God.

The spirituality of authority, then, is a spirituality based on listening to those around me. The monastic listens to the gospel and to privileged others—the prioress, the children, the spouse, the management—and to the Rule and to life around them. The monastic listens, and listens, and listens. The monastic listens to God, to the community, to the world in order to grow beyond the limits that clamor for satisfaction in the confusion of wants and whims.

Monastic spirituality rejects a static concept of perfection. Perfection, the monastic learns, is not something that has to do with seeing a commitment to obedience and authority as a variation on life in a military barracks. On the contrary, the monastic learns young to realize that the whole of life must be open to the possibility of change, always and everywhere, because God cannot be defined by yesterday. God is constantly revealing the fullness of God, more today than yesterday, more tomorrow than today. To find God, then, we must be always ready to bend our hearts and change our paths and open our minds. That's why dependence is static and license is blind. And that's why domination is destructive.

The third negative view of authority, domination, says there is only one right way, mine. Worse than that, domination says that I have nothing to learn from anyone else and that you have nothing to teach me. The person who attempts to dominate others has great gaping human needs for security and control. If the world does not go together the way I want it, then the world is wrong. I want this schedule and this menu and this arrangement.

Anything other is less than perfect. But that's a crippled and smothered way to live. It cuts off surprise. It stunts growth. It eliminates the need for the future. It says that whatever the world is, it is frozen.

What's more, the function of domination is to keep the rest of the world small as well. No one else is allowed to have vision either. No one else is permitted to fail. No one else is given the opportunity to learn by experience. The world is to step to my beat. Everybody else exists for me. My wife is to make my life comfortable. My husband is there to give me status and make me feel important. My friend is supposed to like what I like, do what I do, think what I think and move when I move.

Domination, in other words, does not direct people, it destroys them. But the Rule of Benedict says, "The Abbot is not to disturb the flock entrusted to him nor make any unjust arrangements, as though he had the power to do whatever he wished" (RB 63). And he said that in a period of Roman patriarchy when men had control over the lives of their children and slaves.

Benedictine spirituality sees authority as a charism, not a privilege. It sees obedience as an act of community, not a deprivation of life or a diminishment of the person. Benedictine spirituality, then, gives the lie to dependence and license and domination. Like the Teacher who tells us that Truth comes from being able to admit that we may be wrong, Benedictine spirituality teaches that dependence or domination or license are not to rule us.

Dependence says that everybody counts but me. License says that nobody counts but me. And domination says that I have the right to tell everybody else what counts at all. It's into those skewed perspectives of life and authority that Benedictine spirituality sheds light and gives new hope.

The Rule of Benedict calls for a life of conversion. One of the Benedictine vows signed on the altar is the vow of *Conversatio Morum*, or a promise to take on a life-style and values and attitudes that are different from the life-style and values and attitudes that permeate the society around us. We are to be gospel people. We are not to be our own law; we are not to be the centers of our own universe; we are not to be unaware, unconcerned, unlistening to all the others. We are to be the formers of human community, and we are to be formed by it as well. That is the function of authority.

Authority is more than the preservation of law or the maintenance of order. Authority is the call to growth.

It is not the function of spouses to control one another. It is not the obligation of parents simply to restrict children. It is not the responsibility of national leaders to restrain the nation. It is the responsibility of the authorities of one generation to develop the people of the next, not to turn them into perpetual children, certified robots, licensed clones.

The Rule of Benedict says quite clearly that the older must love the younger, that the young must honor their elders, that authority must be delegated (RB 71). Advice must be taken from the entire group "starting with the youngest members first" (RB 3:10). This teaches newer members not to be inhibited or nonresponsive or unconcerned, perhaps, but the structure was also designed to let the young hear their more experienced elders reflect aloud on the fresh and untried opinions they so eagerly gave. As the young listen, their own ideas and understandings are sharpened in preparation for the day when the generation yet to come is their responsibility.

The Rule says the responsibility of the abbot is to study the Scriptures so that he can "bring forth both new things and old" (RB 64:8). The role of the authority in monastic spirituality is clear: Authority is meant to call. Authority is meant to enable. Authority is meant to raise questions. Authority is meant to convert. Authority is meant to shape us in the values of Christian life. Authority wielded in any other manner is not authority at all, it is sheer egotism and potential tyranny. There is no room in Benedictine spirituality for the domineering father or the overprotective mother or the prima donna director. Authority is the tool that is meant to lead us all to the fullness of self that is rooted in the fullness of community.

By recognizing authorities in our lives we run the risk of conversion, of learning from someone else. Conversion says that creation goes on creating and that none of us are meant to thwart the dynamic character of the Christian life. In every century, of course, someone tries. After the revolutions, there were those who tried to restore the monarchies; after Vatican II, there were those who would have preferred to live in the spirit of Vatican I; after the rise of the women's movement, there were those who wanted to restore the patriarchal family. And all in the name of authority. But the authority that leads to conversion is always an authority that calls us beyond a limited present to a life of new gospel insights and new possibilities.

Conversion, in other words, is a willingness to let go, to be led beyond where we are, to where we can be. Conversion is an invitation not to cling to past works, to past relationships, to past circumstances. Those are the idols of our lives; those are the places where we have paused along the way. Conversion opens us to new questions.

Conversion, then, demands self-discipline; it presumes struggle; it needs the guidance of authority. Someplace, sometime, we have to learn to trust that the direction authority gives and the questions authority raises and the call to growth that authority inspires is a call to the fulfillment of the self, not an exercise in servility for its own sake.

Those are good words for parents, important words for institutions, decisive words for nations, and determining words for the Church. What we need in our times are spiritual adults. Dependence, license, and domination, the Teacher knew well, are no substitutes for the self-contained, self-controlled, self-directed person who can withstand the vagaries of life and not crumble, who can withstand the pressures of life and not succumb, who can regard the forces of life and not be seduced by anything less than self brought to maturity and community brought to wholeness. We each have something to offer and offer it we must.

That's what the spirituality of Benedictine authority is all about, and that's what family life, the country, and the Church need more now in our time than ever. To allow ourselves to be other in the name of obedience to any authority that would lead us to be less is to betray them all.

"Listen with the heart" (RB Prologue: 1), the Rule of Benedict says. Listen with feeling and listen with compassion. Listen with values and listen with concern. Listen for the truth of a thing, not for the power of a thing. Obey what makes your heart more human, not necessarily what makes your position more secure. Listen with a critical ear for the sound of the gospel in everything you do. And don't do what isn't a gospel act, no matter who says so, no matter who orders it, no matter how sacred the institution that demands it. Or else the Holocaust. Or else the Inquisition. Or else Watergate and Irangate. Or else power before truth.

The modern world is a battleground between dependence and authority, between license and authority, between domination and real authority. Benedictine spirituality insists that blind obedience, obedience to the lawgiver rather than to the law, is the lowest form of service. And Benedictine spirituality is a standard for lawgivers too. Benedictine authority is authority full of respect and full of humility, open to questions and intent on vision, intent on growth rather than on control.

The world and its families, the nations and their peoples have never needed a Benedictine spirituality of authority more.

12

Stability: Revelation of the Many Faces of God

The workshop where we are to toil faithfully at all these tasks is the enclosure of the monastery and stability in the community.

When one is to be received, they come before the whole community in the oratory and promise stability, fidelity to monastic life, and obedience.

RB 4:78; 58:17

Everywhere you look in our monastery there's a cross: on the bell tower outside the large front entrance for all the world to see; on the chapel doors; on the wall behind the prioress's desk. When I was a young sister in the community, I think I would have preferred more exciting markers—an elegant oil painting, perhaps, or a statue of the Ascension done in gothic beauty, or something abstract and provocative. Not that there weren't plenty of each around, of course, but the first sight a visitor got was always the cross; the most prominent thing was always the cross; the thing at the center of the most symbolic places of the community— the front door, the chapel, the refectory, the prioress's office—was always the cross. A little old-fashioned, I thought. A little macabre. After all, we have to keep our eyes on the bright spots of life and beware the darker aspects of religion. And I still think that's true. To a point.

The fact is, though, that as life goes on, it becomes clearer and clearer that the cross is not a dark aspect of religion. It is, on the contrary, the one hope we have that our own lives can move through difficulty to triumph. It's the one thing that enables us to hang on and not give up when hanging on seems impossible and giving up seems imperative. The cross is our one proof of human possibility. The cross says very clearly that things will work out if we work them out and that whatever is, is important to our life's fulfillment. The cross says that we can rise if we can only endure.

Now that is not what I learn from the culture around me. In this day and age everything is expected to be instant, nothing is to be endured. We're a society of pop-up tarts and instant cocoa and microwave ovens and same day surgery. Americans are instructed that they must never tolerate a cold or a backache or acid indigestion. And we want things when we want them. We wear headphones to create our own private little worlds. We run our lives on timers for the VCR and timers for the lights and timers for the oven in order to create our own private little schedules. We buy TV dinners so everyone in the family can live their own private little lives. We change schools and jobs and homes as casually as we once changed clothes. We are born in one state, raised in another, married in a third, and retire in a fourth. Everything we touch is immediate, private, and fluid. Life, for us, is very, very personal and very, very mobile. Our lives are so mobile and so private, in fact, that loneliness and fragmentation and selfishness are endemic to the culture. We "mind our own business" while people cheat and lie and die around us. We fail to make connections between this little suburb and the world, my life and the health of the planet, this policy and the fate of ages and peoples yet to come.

When my novice mistress insisted that nothing be left on the novitiate table overnight, I didn't make many connections either. When I was assigned to live with people I didn't know, I didn't understand why connecting with them was important to me either. When my first local superior gave each of us one hanger and one hanger only in the community cupboard, I didn't understand why my needs didn't determine the allotment either. When I was told to work with people whose methods I didn't understand and whose personalities countered mine, I didn't know why it was necessary for me to have anything to do with them either. When we were told that typewriters could not be used in the bedroom areas, I didn't see why they shouldn't be either. After all, I had grown up an only child. The world around me belonged to me. Things went my way if only because there was no other way for anything to go. The turf was mine to own and shape and control. I was a world unto myself, all others need beware.

Then, as the years went by, I began to understand the spirituality of stability that was so clearly a monastic quality. The Desert Monastics explained it this way:

Abba Poemen said of Abba John that he had prayed to God to take his passions away from him so that he might become free from care. In fact, Abba John went and told one of the elders this: "I find myself in peace, without an enemy," he said. And the elder said to him, "Then go and beseech God to stir up warfare within you so that you may regain the affliction and humility that you used to have, for it is by warfare that the soul makes progress." So he besought God and when warfare came, he no longer prayed that it might be taken away, but said, "Lord, give me the strength for the fight" (John the Dwarf, section no. 13.).

Another story that reflects the spirituality of stability comes from Cassian. Cassian wrote that Abba John, abbot of a great monastery, went to Abba Paesius who had been living for forty years very far off in the desert. As John was very fond of Paesius and could therefore speak freely with him, John said to him, "What good have you done by living here in retreat for so long, and not being easily disturbed by anyone?" And Abba Paesius said, "Since I have lived in solitude the sun has never seen me eating." But Abba John said to him, "As for me, as long as I have lived in community, the sun has never seen me angry" (Cassian, section no. 4.).

It is easy to be even-tempered in private, in other words. It is easy to be virtuous alone. It is easy to be strong when untried. It is easy to win when there is nothing to endure. It is also easy to be superficial and self-centered and characterless. It is also easy to run from what I may most need to confront in life if I am ever to be whole. Monastic stability, you see, is concerned more with depth than with comfort.

Benedictine stability is a promise to meet life head-on. Monastic stability deals directly with three things: centeredness, commitment, and relationships.

There are some things in life that cannot be avoided: death, illness, change, personal expectations. What each of them does to us depends a great deal on the way we have allowed ourselves to deal with lesser things. The purpose of stability is to center us in something greater than ourselves so that nothing lesser than ourselves can possibly sweep us away.

Stability says that where I am is where God is for me. More than that, stability teaches that whatever the depth of the dullness or the difficulties around me, I can, if I will simply stay still enough of heart, find God there in the midst of them.

Mobility tempts interior stillness to the breaking point, however. Every store window holds a better bargain. Every relationship promises a more satisfying partnership. Every new place and new person and new possibility tempts me to try again, to try over, to try once more to find the perfect place or at least the place perfectly suited to me. But centeredness is an antidote to the fragmentation that comes from never settling in to where I am or what I'm doing or what I'm meant to learn.

When the monastic makes a vow of stability it is a vow designed to still the wandering heart. There comes a time in life when everyone else's family seems to have been better than my own. There comes a moment when having everything seems to be the only way to squeeze even a little out of life. There comes a day when this job, this home, this town, this family all seem irritating and deficient beyond the bearable. There comes a period in life when I regret every major decision I've ever made. That is precisely the time when the spirituality of stability offers its greatest gift. Stability enables me to outlast the dark, cold places of life until the thaw comes and I can see new life in this uninhabitable place again. But for that to happen I must learn to wait through the winters of my life.

The problem is that perseverance and persistence are aspects of stability which the present world counts little.

If our children don't learn, we blame the teachers rather than expect the students to study harder. If the book is difficult, we don't read it even if the intellectual struggle would be worth it. If the show is too long, we leave early even if that wastes the price of the ticket. If the work is hard, we quit. Stability, however, says that we have an obligation to see things through until we have done for them what can be done and, no less important, until they have done for us what can be done as well.

Stability says we will walk the major roads of life unto the end, no matter what. There is, of course, a kind of pseudostability that is destructive. To fail to move out of situations that are unjust or demeaning or depersonalizing simply because I cannot find the courage to take the step is not stability. That kind of rootedness is a kind of bondage or suicide that comes from inertia, or entrapment, or a love of pain that betrays some twisted need for sympathy or pity or false martyrdom. Stability says that we stay with a thing in order to grow, not in order not to grow. Fidelity is to be valued, of course, but not at the cost of mental health. Humility is to be valued, indeed, but not if it implies becoming masochistic. Prayer is to be valued, certainly, but not instead of responsibility to others. Stability says there are some values beyond other values that ought to be pursued.

Stability says we will stay with the humdrum if only to condition our souls to cope with the unfleeable in life. We stay with what, if we wanted to, we really could get away from so that we can come someday to cope with what we will not be able to leave.

Stability requires us to be constant of heart and unremitting in our spiritual efforts. We don't pray in hope of visions; we pray in hope of becoming prayerful. We don't struggle in hope of triumph; we struggle in hope of growth. We don't continue in hope of winning trophies; we continue in hope of winning the struggle to become better and stronger human beings than we were. If this is a thing worth doing, then I must do it. If this is a cause to which I can make a contribution, then I must make it. If this is a promise that needs keeping, then you must be able to count on my keeping it.

Commitment, however, is not necessarily our long suit these days. Nothing in this society requires it and everything militates against it. It is not expected, after all, to promise to stay at a thing when something bad happens to it or something seemingly better comes along. It is not easy to continue the hard work of being here when everything around us says go there where it will be easier. It is hard to go on when it would be so much simpler just to quit. But the question becomes, what will happen to me as a person if I don't go on, if I don't persevere, if I don't persist, if I don't see this through? The answers are myriad.

In the first place, I will certainly fail to learn a great deal about myself if I leave a thing before it's finished. I will fail to learn the strengths that give me quality. And I will fail to face the weaknesses that call for change. I will end up being less than I can be. It is the image of Robert E. Perry stopping just one hundred miles away from the North Pole that tarnishes his image more, for instance, than if he'd never gone at all.

In the second place, I will lose the opportunity to grow. Stability is the quality that enables me to confront life's questions with both self-knowledge and self-giving. Not every question reveals itself at once. Not every effort succeeds at first attempt. Not every good thing that happens, happens without persistent purpose and continual failure. After Vatican II, for instance, religious life, parish life, and personal morality took erratic swings. People stopped going to church. Men and women left their religious communities. Some went the way of the past in order to maintain direction; others launched out into a chaotic present without map and without caution. Not a few left the spiritual life altogether. The critics said that God was dead, that religious life was over, that the Church had lost meaning. But there has never been a more exciting time, a more hopeful time, a more important time for followers of the gospel than now. Now spirituality has become a gift rather than a social expectation. For those for whom staying with the struggle demanded conscious commitment to faith alone, religion has taken on a meaning beyond itself. Indeed, the search for purpose and meaning and relevance has often become skewed these years and has seldom been clear. It has nevertheless managed to remain very, very important. The staying through itself, in fact, has often been the best part of the spiritual gift. The dark night of faith can be its own kind of blessing, just as staying through a relationship or staying through a crisis or staying through an illness can be a gift, too, if we stay for no other reason than to discover with open minds and accepting hearts who we are and what we are expected to give and to learn in this situation.

To those who are pure of heart, to those who come to see God where God is, to those who persevere in the presence of God, to those who, as the Rule of Benedict says, "have used the spiritual craft without ceasing day and night" (RB 4:75–76) is promised the reward of a loving God: peace of heart and eternal life at the end of whatever daily deaths crowd our lives.

Stability, in other words, is an outward demonstration of what we say is our inward disposition: the love of God in all things but especially in the humdrum and mundane, in the here and now and the them and those.

Obviously, then, stability has to be more than centeredness and commitment. Stability must most of all be the sanctification of relationships, the discovery of friendship where perhaps once only chemistry had been. The fact is that stability is an invitation to live life deeply rather than to spend it superficially. The temptation to flit from person to person, from commitment to commitment, from place to place in a mobile society is of very modern making. Our ancestors stayed with one job for a lifetime. They lived in their hometowns all their lives. Choice was not a luxury they had. Stability was their way of life.

But modern society has lost that essential call to the depth and conversion that comes from knowing everyone and having everyone know you. Now we confuse community with living in groups. Yet lots of people who seem to be living with others are simply living alone together. People live in the same neighborhood together for years and cannot even call one another by name. People work for the same company all their lives and never even see one another. People go to the same schools together and never even know it. Indeed our lives are lived on the suburban surface of things, not in community at all.

Ongoing revelation of God's goodness depends somehow, though, on permanence, on realizing that God's action in my life is different today from what it was yesterday and realizing that my actions in life are different today from what they were yesterday. To test and try all those dimensions of life takes time. It is one thing to speak kindly to an irritating stranger on Monday. It is quite another thing to go on speaking kindly to the same irritating relative, or irritating employee, or irritating child day after day, week after week, year after year and come to see in that what God is asking of me, what God is teaching me about myself in this weary, weary moment.

What enables a person to keep going back to the difficult parts of life is, inevitably, certitude in the faithfulness of God. I do not keep the promises I've made, the contracts I've signed, the guarantees I've given because I am sure of my strength. I go on keeping covenants that would be easy to forego only because I am sure of the constancy of God. I am sure that God will keep God's promises of presence and grace. I feed my ailing mother every day because I am convinced that God is God. I patch and patch and patch this marriage together because I have no doubt that God is God. I go on hoping in this difficult child because I am convinced that God is God. I continue to pray when prayer itself is a burden because I am certain that God is God. It is not myself and my own strength and my own fidelity in which I put my hope. I put my hope in the certain, the guaranteed, the gracious faithfulness of God. That's what makes stability possible. That's what makes stability imperative.

Stability, you see, is essential to the ongoing revelation of the many faces of God in my life. Someday, somehow I have to see a thing through to the end or I will never come to know what I was meant to find there and I will never come to recognize the face of God that is hidden there and I will never come to be all that I could be there.

Stability is what gives me time in life, time for God and time for others. If I rush from job to job and city to city and relationship to relationship, I never discover all the aspects of each. I never find the rhythm of life. I never touch all the dimensions of anything. I never get stretched beyond myself. I never become bonded to others. I never become something new. And alienation sets in.

Then, finally, it becomes clear. Mobility is not the ultimate enemy of stability, alienation is. When nothing has touched me deeply enough to change me, nothing can touch me at all. I become a cardboard cutout that breathes. I learn to say the proper words, perhaps, but I never learn the grace that comes from anger suffered but not spat out, or pain borne but not denied, or love learned but never able to be expressed. I go through life on fast speed but numb.

The Benedictine spirituality of stability is the antithesis of that. The Rule calls for steady, steady attention to everything: to prayer, to the service of the other, to the community as a whole, to regularity and continuity and manual labor and intellectual discipline, to "love of one another with chaste love" (RB 72:8). No one is excused from any of them. Life is a package to be opened in its entirety, not a smorgasbord to be sampled as it suits us.

If there is anything, in fact, that reminds me that I am not a world unto myself, it is stability in my community: "the school of the Lord's service," "the workshop where I work out the spiritual craft" (RB 4). Stability implies both acceptance of the human community in which I find myself and immersion in it.

It is so easy for people to come to live with others as if they were living alone. All they have to do is to stop noticing one another. But that is not a spiritual community at all. I need the conscious presence of other people to become sensitive to God's presence, to hear the gospel

Word in life through those who are speaking it around me, and to be able to express my love for Christ in a real way, in the other, in the world. Stability is the one sure tool we have to be certain that the world, for us, can really become a garden to be tilled rather than a candy store to be robbed.

Stability, the willingness to continue to grow where I am, ironically, is the ground of conversion, the willingness to be changed. With these people, in this place, at this time I dedicate myself to rebirth and growth and maturity, both spiritual and psychological. With the help of these others, I can commit myself to the faithfulness of a God who is also unpredictable.

Stability is a measure of love as well. Here in a stable relationship with others, we find that fullness of life is more than preservation of the self and that love is more than a matter of physical response, more than a mixture of fire and dynamite. It's in stability that I find out that all love, to be true love, must, at least to some degree, be celibate. For love to be more than a passing mixture of fire and dynamite, it must come to withstand the days of no fire or dynamite at all. It must to some degree be more than sexual attraction and beyond sexual attraction. It must be made of friendship and mutual respect and spiritual integrity, or staying through will not only be impossible, it will be destructive. Friendship, in other words, is the call out of isolation and selfishness in order to teach me how to love and how to serve. But without stability, friendship—real soul-searing friendship, the kind that makes us choose between domination and infatuation and possessiveness and dependence for growth and freedom and depth and responsibility and self-knowledge—is impossible.

Stability is what enables us, in other words, to live totally in God and totally for others. It is those two quests in life, in fact, that may be our only counterweights to pathological egotism in this self-centered world where whole nations can starve to death on our kitchen TV sets while we eat supper without even so much as raising an eyebrow about it all. What else can explain human callousness of that proportion except the lack of human caring that comes only from living through things with people? What else can possibly have led the human race to accept the prospect of nuclear annihilation in the name of "defense" if not the distances that have grown up between our worlds and the lives of those around us as we come and go and come and go through life, unrooted, unknown, and unattached?

Is stability easy? Not on your life. But as the Desert Monastics told us, "It is by warfare that the soul makes progress." And if, by living as responsible members of the human community, we can come to the point where "the sun never sees our anger," then we will have come to fullness of life.

That's why, I have discovered after years of monastic life, there are crosses in those four particular places in the monastery: on the bell tower above the building to raise our hearts and efforts to levels beyond the mundane; on the chapel doors so that I can remember what life is really all about; on the refectory wall to make visible the gift of personal growth that community gives; over the prioress's desk so that I can see the divine behind the human everywhere in life. That's what those crosses say every time I see them: Stability. Stability. Stability. Stability.

13

Monastic Practices: The Way of Conversion

These, then, are the tools of the spiritual craft. When we have used them without ceasing day and night and have returned them on judgment day, our wages will be the reward God has promised: "What the eye has not seen nor the ear heard, God has prepared for those who love him" (1 Cor. 2:9).

RB 4:75–78

My novice mistress and I did not always see eye to eye. She wanted silence when I was laughing. She wanted lights out when I wanted to study. She wanted unquestioning obedience when I wanted to discuss a thing. She expected fasting when I wanted an orange between meals. She wanted intense effort on things I would have preferred to treat once-over lightly. Now let there be no doubt: her way always won the day, but there is an enormous amount of difference between doing a thing and understanding it. And I thought I'd never understand it at all. As much as I loved monastic life, it seemed that everything was rigor and ritual, that there was no time here for the person, for the human, for the real. On the contrary.

I would have understood better, I think, if I had just

given a bit more thought to the practice of the receiving of the Rule and the receiving of the breviary. When I entered, I was given three books and three books only: the Rule of Benedict, the breviary, and the Book of Community Customs.

The Rule was to enable us to transcend community to achieve union with God.

The breviary was to enable us to pray with the community.

The customs book was to enable us to live with the community. .

The Rule wasn't all that clear. The breviary I could navigate with the help of the novices who marked every section of the Divine Office for us every day. And the customs book I understood only too well: the sisters were to leave the chapel in rank; the sisters were to keep their arms crossed under their scapulars; the sisters were to bow to the crucifix upon entering the refectory. The list of prescriptions was endless. It was an entire manual on how to bow and how to sit and how to organize the day and how to talk to the prioress and how to walk through the halls. The customs book covered everything in life, it seemed, and for a long time I considered it a lot more important than the Rule.

As the years went by, though, the advantages of holding my hands just so, the tricks of walking lightly, and the niceties of bowing took their proper places in the lexicon of rubrics and ritual that made up days that were divided among the liturgical, the professional, and the contemplative dimensions of life. Then, too, the endless list of community conventions that were detailed in the formation program became unmasked for what they were: the requirements of any organized institution, the hallmarks of any well-ordered spiritual life lived in common. Finally I began to realize that the essential elements of monastic spirituality were in the Rule itself. The chapter is entitled, appropriately enough, "On the Instruments of Good Works." It was there that I began to discover that there really are disciplines that guard the heart and open the soul to the Holy. The Desert Monastics explained it this way:

> It was said of Abba Isaiah that one day he took a branch and went to the threshing-floor to thresh and said to the owner, "Give me some wheat." And the owner replied, "Well, have you brought in the harvest, Father?" And Abba Isaiah said, "No." So the owner said to him, "How then can you expect to be given wheat, if you have not harvested?" Then the old man said to him, "Are you saying then that if someone does not work, they do not receive wages?" And the owner said, "Of course I am." So the old man went away.
>
> Seeing what he had done, the monastics of that place bowed before him, asking him to tell them why he had acted in that way. And the old man said to them, "I did this as an example: whoever has not worked will not receive a reward from God."

My novice mistress was right after all. The spiritual life was something to be worked at, not something to be hoped for. Working at it required discipline and monastic mindfulness.

The question is, How can mindfulness possibly be achieved in the midst of a life full of pressure and full of care? The "Instruments of Good Works" are clear. The point of a Benedictine spirituality is not to make life unusual, not to make life strange or foreign or rigid or mysterious. The purpose of Benedictine spirituality is to make life significant and sacred and full of meaning. If I want to live in the presence of God, there are some preparations to be made. The basic questions of the spiritual life are to determine which ones and how?

The secret, of course, lies in the Benedictine commitment to conversion. I cannot serve God and mammon, I cannot serve two masters, I cannot be both in the world and of it. I cannot have an authentic spiritual life without working at it. The spiritual life is not a matter of religious sleight of hand. It is not the doing of spiritual tricks that we are about. It is an attitude of mind we must develop. It is a way of walking lightly through things that threaten to bind us or bog us down—that is what a true spirituality implies. It is an asceticism without chains.

The shock comes when we finally realize that spirituality itself can be a temptation. Benedict speaks clearly about "the evil zeal of bitterness which separates from God and leads to hell" (RB 72:1) and the pitfall of wishing "to be called holy before we are holy" (RB 4:62). The Rule, in other words, teaches us to cling to nothing, to hold everything—even the best of holy things—with a relaxed grasp.

The great problem of the spiritual life, I soon learned, was not the problem of choosing good from bad. Learning to choose good from bad was, in fact, deceptively easy. There are few who steal, few who lie. There are not too many of us with uncontrollable tempers or destructive jealousies. Most of us would walk away from a fight or refuse to cheat the company or beware of the neighborhood gossip. Those things are easy to see as unholy and clear to avoid. No, I soon learned, the real problem of the spiritual life was not rooted in having to learn to avoid evil and choose good; the real problem lay in having to learn to choose good from good. Faced with receiving the unexpected guest and going to prayer, which is better? Confronted with the possibility of making life more comfortable and living it more simply, which is better? Awash in the choice between authority and conscience, which is truly most gospel? Those are the great spiritual decisions. More than that, if we ever do get the choices right, how do we keep them right? How do we establish a family prayer life when the family keeps growing through different schedules at different times? How do we keep giving to charity when our own household has growing wants? How do we deal with the nuclear issue when the company we work for is tied into military contracts and we're too old to make a job change?

What does the Rule of Benedict have to say to those things, to the problems of living a spiritual life in a materialistic world? How do we build community in a world that is immersed in itself? What, in other words, is Benedictine asceticism?

What makes the spiritual life different from any other life? What are we doing that is so different from what everybody else is doing? The answer is it is not what we are doing at all that makes the spiritual life different from the life lived without consciousness. The answer is it is what we are and how we do what we do that is the mark of the spiritual life. It is what we are while we are doing whatever it is we do that makes Benedictine spirituality a gift for all ages.

When we were young in the community, we were taught to make a bow of the head to everyone we passed in the corridor, not in order to say hello as I had originally assumed, but to recognize the presence of God in them. Elders went through doorways first, not because they were older, but because we were being taught to recognize the guidance available in experience. No one was to have more than three habits and two pairs of shoes, not to play games with the notion of religious poverty— God knows we could easily have all managed to amass more—but to teach us the principle of sufficiency. After awhile, however, the messages, great as they were, got lost in the mechanics of it all because mechanics are not Benedictine. This is precisely the way to say the Office, chapters of Rule imply, but then those chapters end with this comment: "However, if anyone knows a better way, let that be done" (RB 18). This is the daily schedule, the Rule teaches, but "let the abbot make whatever arrangements suit best" (RB 47). See that every monastic has the following personal supplies, the Rule itemizes, and then instructs, "Let those who need more, ask" (RB 55). Clearly the Benedictine life is about a great deal more than lists of community behaviors or daily activities.

Why no checklist of prioritized virtues or stylized behaviors or rigid rules to accompany spiritual development according to the Rule of Benedict? The answer is simple: "conversion" is more important to the mind of Benedict than captivity to a system, and, in fact, a spiritual system is often a mask for conversion, an avoidance of conversion. Conversion requires us to grow and to change. Systems too easily lock us into yesterday's virtues.

So there, without so much as a philosophical explanation or an introduction, in the fourth chapter of the Rule called "The Instruments of Good Works," Benedict identifies the dimensions of Benedictine life that lead to conversion of heart and breadth of soul and depth of insight and richness of life. The instruments of good works, it seems to me, cover three distinct categories. These are the Benedictine practices of asceticism: the Ten Commandments and the spiritual and corporal works of mercy (RB 4:1–21); the elements of community life (RB 4:22–33); and a commitment to personal maturity (RB 4:34–62).

The commandments of God and the spiritual and corporal works of mercy move us beyond the kind of rarefied atmosphere of canned Christianity so often incorrectly identified with the spiritual life. The spiritual life is a call to live the Christian life well, not simply by denying ourselves or removing ourselves from the vortex of life to follow Christ, as necessary as that is, but also by reaching out to others. The spiritual life is not a matter of not doing evil to the other; the real spiritual life depends on our doing good for the other. If Benedictine spirituality demands that I "relieve the poor and clothe the naked and visit the sick and console the sorrowing" (RB 4:14–18), then my spiritual life is incomplete as long as I make subsidized housing and soup kitchens and AIDS victims and refugees no business of mine. Prayer is simply not enough.

Benedictine spirituality, in other words, is a spirituality of cosmic connectedness. Time, land, people, things are all to be held in reverent hands, all to be seen as vehicles of the Holy.

In the second category of the "Instruments of Good Works," Benedict puts those concepts that enable us to be good community and family members. We are told not to give way to anger, not to plot revenge, not to live a life of deceit, not to be unkind, not to hate our enemies though clearly enemies we may have, not to lack patience and forbearance in times of stress.

It is such a different approach from the one being presented in the name of me-ness. The Me Generation has learned to "get its anger out," "to win by intimidation," to "take care of Number One," to "nuke the Russians," to "demand our rights," to sue our parents and cheat our bosses and get our way, whatever it takes. And when it's all over, we pay money these days to have psychologists and psychiatrists point out to us that the raging angers we harbor and the roles we play and the subterfuges we plan do a great deal more damage to ourselves than they ever do to the people on whom we wreak them. Benedictine spirituality says we just can't be whole, we just can't be free, we just can't be happy, and we just can't build the very community life we want, personal and private or global and grand, until we put the self down. Benedictine spirituality says that we cannot make ourselves our only life agenda. Monastic spirituality softens us. Benedictine spirituality, in other words, says we must learn to live in the midst of the human struggle with quiet souls and open hearts. For the Benedictine, life in community is the great human asceticism. To live community life well is to have all the edges rubbed off, all the rough parts made smooth. There is no need then for disciplines to practice. Life itself is the discipline.

The third category of the "Instruments of Good Works" is broader still. These are the instruments concerned with personal maturity and spiritual growth (RB 4:34–62). Here we're told not to be proud or intent on control, to resist addictions, to use our energies well, to avoid negative thoughts and negative speech patterns, to recognize our own creaturehood, to nourish the interior life, to live life with seriousness of purpose and a consciousness of ultimate things, to reach out to others, to love with a love that is nonexploitative, to be a healing presence, and, finally, when we fail and fail and fail in all of these, never to despair. We are being told in a document fifteen hundred years old what any good psychologist, any gentle healer of souls would say today: live life for something greater than your satisfactions and do not let anything or anyone cause you to lose hold on your free and unfettered self.

Benedictine asceticism is scriptural and communal and committed to psychological and spiritual adulthood. To develop a Benedictine spirituality means to reject a static concept of perfection in which keeping the rules and going through the motions is, at best, an easy way. Benedictine spirituality plunges me into human relations that are meant to reveal the will of God to me, to call forth the best in me, to be a source of support and a measure of my personal responsibility. Perhaps the best test of the reality of these in my life is a simple question: In the last three things that bothered me this week, whom did I blame and was it really worth the emotional energy I gave to it? It is time to realize that it is not what happens to me in life that counts, it is what I do with what happens to me that is the measure of my happiness. For some people, life is a challenge; for others, life is a continual crisis, the resolution of which is someone else's responsibility.

Benedictine conversion, then, is not an assertion of our strength or character. Benedictine spirituality is based on the simple acknowledgment that God will come to life before us and be reborn in us in unexpected ways day after day throughout our entire lives. We must be ready to respond to this God of woods and highways, of gentle breeze and cataclysm, of privacy and crowds—however this Spirit comes. Response is the essence of Benedictine spirituality.

It is out of this desire to be attentive and present and ready that the externals of monastic spirituality arise as well. As Abba Isaiah meant to point out to the disciples of that day, there are works that for centuries have prepared the monastic mind for the harvest, that without which there may be no harvest at all. For the Benedictine silence, custom, the common table, *statio*, *lectio*, manual labor, and stewardship are the tools of the spiritual craft.

Silence is an element of monastic spirituality that begs for rediscovery in our time. Muzak fills our elevators. Hard rock blares out of cars and boats and apartment house windows. People jog down highways with earphones on and bicycle along city streets balancing boom boxes on their handlebars and sit in airports with transistor radios against their ears, all of them insulated against the world around them and, most of all, protected against the searchings within themselves. Monastic spirituality says we must learn to listen to the cacophony within us in order to defy its demands and to dampen its hold on us.

Monastic spirituality says it is the clamor of the self that needs to be brought to quiet so that the quiet of God can be brought to consciousness. Monastic spirituality says it is the cry of our own passions that mute the cry of others. Monastic spirituality says people who cannot live comfortably with silence can never live comfortably with noise.

But silence is a frightening thing. Silence leaves us at the mercy of the noise within us. We hear the fears that need to be faced. We hear, then, the angers that need to be cooled. We hear the emptiness that needs to be filled. We hear the cries for humility and reconciliation and centeredness. We hear ambition and arrogance and attitudes of uncaring awash in the shallows of the soul. Silence demands answers. Silence invites us to depth. Silence heals what hoarding and running will not touch.

So, monastic spirituality calls us to live quietly: to walk

calmly rather than to run; to turn doorknobs rather than to push doors shut; to speak to a person directly rather than to shout down halls at them; to turn sound down rather than up; to avoid noise pollution; to give the gift of silence to others.

Monastic spirituality calls us to learn to live easily with ourselves. Monastic spirituality calls us, too, to learn to step quietly and consciously into the presence of God, listening and waiting and trusting.

Life without silent space is not life at all. If we're accustomed to leave the TV on in empty rooms while we work to the blur of the sounds it siphons through the house or we can't wash dishes without the radio playing; if we're never alone for a minute of the day and we never just stand and watch a flower grow; if we can't drive across town without the car tape recorder blaring and if sitting in a chair in silence for thirty minutes a day simply thinking, thinking, thinking is one of the more painful possibilities we can imagine, then silence may be exactly what we need to wash away the frenetic energy of life and still its storms.

One thing is sure: without some semblance of silence everyday, there can be no such thing as monastic spirituality at all. "Monastics should diligently cultivate silence at all times," the Rule writes, "and especially at night" (RB 42:1). Especially at night we should bring the day to a centered close and listen inside to what it did to us and set about hearing its lessons and listening to its Word made flesh in us. Out of silence, the Rule implies, comes gentleness and patience and good work and seriousness of purpose and consciousness of the essence of life.

Imagine what would happen in this country if children did not come from homes where families screamed at one another from morning dawn until the last hour of night. Imagine what the cities would be like if boom boxes did not blast and thump from every midnight to every dawn. Imagine what our souls would be like if the last thought we thought at night did not come to us from the local TV. Imagine what our lives and work and relationships would be like if they were not crowded with noise and simmering with agitation.

Monastic silence is an antidote to the turmoil that is manufactured to distract us from the important things of life. Without silence, monastic spirituality cannot leaven the soul.

But silence is not the only tool of the spiritual craft that is an auxiliary to Benedictine spirituality. Community customs are monastic practices designed to weld the community in the faith that unites them and to bring mindfulness even to the most mundane activities of life. When I was a young woman in the community, one of our customs was to break the bread on our dinner plates into three pieces at every meal in order to call to mind the three persons of the Trinity and to rest the dinner knives beside our serving plates on one of them in recollection of the cross. As we walked through the halls, we crossed our hands under our scapulars in tribute to Jesus bound. We bowed to the crucifix as we left the dining room. We called our bedrooms our "cells." We took new names when we entered the novitiate to signify our change of life. We wore uniforms from a different century to indicate our commitment to this time-tried monastic way of life.

Well, times have changed and new customs have sprung up to reflect them. It is our community custom now, for instance, to go from place to place in the monastery together every New Year, carrying incense and holy water, singing hymns and saying prayers, blessing the house. The custom itself is not original, of course, but the ritual which now surrounds it is. When I was a novice, it was the chaplain who went from door to door sprinkling holy water throughout our halls and saying the prayers while we went right on with our daily work. Now the entire community, led by the prioress, processes from the infirmary, to the bedroom area, to the community room, to the dining room, to the chapel foyer to pray that this year our aging process, our private selves, our community gatherings, and our guests will all be filled with peace in this place.

We do the same thing on Christmas Eve at the blessing of the Christmas crib to remind ourselves that Christmas is not really Christmas until the Christ is born again in each of our lives and in the community as a whole. At the end of every recitation of the Divine Office, the community prayer periods together, the prioress blesses the community itself to remind us of God's everlasting presence with us and our obligation to be a chosen people.

The lighting of the candles of the Advent wreath, the bowing at the "Glory be," the daily remembrance in community prayer of both the sister next to die and the sisters who died on this day since the founding of the community in 1856, the conferences of the prioress, the gathering for community study days three times a year, the daily reading of the Rule and Constitutions, the annual community giveaway of accumulated clothing and materials to the poor, the distribution by the prioress of common readings for Lent, the creation of a common clothes rack where clothing donated to the sisters from local families is placed to be chosen at will by community members, are all community customs designed to make monastic values of community, simplicity, study, humility, poverty, and prayer explicit in our daily lives. Community customs are what make the family, family. They are things done together that tell us who we are together.

They tell us what we stand for and where we draw our energies from and why we go on from day to day. They tell us that over the years, though everything has changed, nothing has really changed at all, not our commitment, not our values, not our life with one another. They tell us that communities grow and change as we each grow and change but that there is a stainless steel underpinning of values and bonds and traditions and purposes that maintain us as we are. They tell us that, surrounded as we are by the trinkets of life, we must learn not to miss what is sacred about it.

People without customs are a rootless people and, often, a blind one. Customs help us to see the natural through the lenses of the Divine. If being at home for Thanksgiving Day is not vastly different from being somewhere else, why bother to go there at all? If there is no way to connect the normal with the wonderful, what can possibly give the little things in life spiritual meaning? The special song and special flower and special prayer and special good-night ritual are the things of which the sacramentality of life are made. It was my mother's custom to sprinkle the house with holy water during heavy electric storms. It was my aunt's custom to mark every family event with a collector's plate. It is a local Polish custom to bless baskets of Easter food before the Easter Vigil. In every instance, the gesture is meant to help us see the connection between the human and the holy.

Community customs, revered and practiced and constantly evolving, are a basic element of a spirituality that sees life as good and earth as the beginning of heaven. It is not so much *what* is done that matters as that *something* is done to raise the ordinary parts of life to signs of life's extraordinary blessings and graces. Benedictine spirituality is awash in customs that keep us moving steadily and surely from one year and one age to the next under the eye of God.

Another tool of the spiritual craft is the common table, a monastic practice of undying tenacity. It is one of the few things in the Rule for which permission to be absent is explicitly required (RB 43). It is one of the few things for which being late is considered an explicit offense (RB 43). The common table in monastic spirituality is no small thing. In Benedictine spirituality, eating is not an act of survival. Eating is an act of community.

The twentieth century understands banquets and fast-food chains, TV dinners and microwave ovens, but the twentieth century does not fully understand the family meal. When schedules get hectic, the family meal is the first thing to go. When plans are being made, being home for dinner is seldom a priority. When work and practice and shopping and meetings get extended, family meals are the first victims. When people live alone, no one gets invited in for dinner.

Benedictine spirituality sees the whole thing differently. The family meal, in the monastic mind-set, is that point of the monastic day when the love and service and self-sacrifice and Word of life that the Eucharist demonstrates in the chapel can be made real again in our personal lives. The act of gathering and sharing and celebrating the day together is the moment when we celebrate one another's gifts to us. Everyone here has made this sustaining moment possible, by preparing the food or paying for the food or growing the food or carrying the food or setting the table for the food or serving the food or cleaning up after the family. Here, at the common table, all our care and work for one another is made tangible.

At the common table, too, is the source of the emotional nourishment and attention for which we all long. When the office is chaotic and the shop is suffocating and the house is unbearable and the organization is neurotic and our friends are disinterested and our acquaintances are unkind, there is always the family table where we will be wanted and attended to and healed of the bad memories of the day. At the common table, the gospel takes on new meaning. Here instructions are given and parables of life are told and miracles of love happen. Here the oldest to the youngest get heard. Here we learn to share: the last piece of pumpkin pie, the one bottle of wine, the recipe and conversation and time. Here are the people who make all the mechanical efforts of taking out the garbage regularly and cutting the grass and dusting the furniture and working overtime worthwhile. Here at the common table we see new life and old, the growing process and the aging process, our failures and our hopes. Here at the common table we remember that all the best work in the world is worth nothing unless it's done for someone.

At the common table, too, we are taught self-control. There is only so much of the vegetables to go around. Everyone must get some. No one must take too much of anything. Nothing should be overcooked. Nothing should be wasted. Nothing that has been prepared for us should be rejected. Here, discipline and fasting are made real.

Here we remember daily those who have none of what we have and recommit our lives to their fulfillment.

Indeed, if there is any indicator at all of the lack of spirituality in American culture it may well be the demise of the family meal and the common table, where privacy has superseded community and personal agendas have come to overshadow the common good. In the meantime, we eat in cars and on stools and in front of cheap TV shows, day after day after day and wonder why we're lonely and why no one cares and why the gospel seems so remote. We open cans instead of peel the tomatoes or clean the corn it would take to make a meal; we eat on the run instead of at a table; we eat alone instead of with someone else and we wonder where the wonders of life have gone. Monastic spirituality says that the wonders of life are all around us and what we must do is to invite people in and learn to revere them.

In addition to silence, community customs, and the common table, the monastic practices of *statio* and *lectio* are also tools of the spiritual craft. *Statio* is a monastic custom that was born centuries ago but clearly belongs in this one. *Statio* is the practice of stopping one thing before we begin another. It is the time between times. It is a cure for the revolving door mentality that is common in a culture that runs on wheels. In monastic spirituality it is common for the community to gather outside of chapel in silence before beginning prayer or at least to gather for a few minutes together in the chapel itself before intoning the opening hymn of the Office.

My novice mistress, in fact, insisted that we all be in chapel five minutes before the bell rang for prayer, an expectation the logic of which managed to elude me for years. After all, "an idle mind is the devil's workshop," the Puritan in me knew well. "Every minute counts," I'd learned somewhere along the way. "Time is golden," the samplers taught. Think of all the things that could have been done in that additional five minutes a day or thirty-five minutes a week or two hours and twenty minutes a month or twenty-eight hours a year: another chapter of typing, another batch of thank you notes composed, another wash ironed, another set of papers corrected. Work, valuable work, could have been done and I could still have made it on time for prayer.

It took years to realize that, indeed, I could have gotten all that work done and still had my body in chapel in time for prayer. It is highly unlikely, though, that my mind would have been there too. The practice of *statio* is meant to center us and make us conscious of what we're about to do and make us present to the God who is present to us. *Statio* is the desire to do consciously what I might otherwise do mechanically. *Statio* is the virtue of presence.

If I am present to this child before I dress her, then the dressing becomes an act of creation. If I am present to my spouse in the living room, then marriage becomes an act of divine communion. If I am present to the flower before I cut it, then life becomes precious. If I am present to the time of prayer before I pray, then prayer becomes the juncture of the human with the Divine.

We have learned well in our time to go through life nonstop. Now it is time to learn to collect ourselves from time to time so that God can touch us in the most hectic of moments.

Statio is the monastic practice that sets out to get our

attention before life goes by in one great blur and God becomes an idea out there somewhere rather than an ever present reality here.

Lectio, or sacred reading, is the monastic practice of keeping our eyes on the transforming moments of life. It may be the centerpiece of all the spiritual arts of the Benedictine tradition and the most necessary for our time of all the pieces of the spiritual craft. The reflective reading of Scripture implies that Scripture was written as much for me as for the Chosen People or the early Christian community. *Lectio* is not so much an attempt to know God in history or Jesus in Israel as much as it is an attempt to know God in my life and Jesus in me.

Our society is full of books and films and videos all designed to show us something or teach us something or help us to escape somewhere. Sacred reading does not set out to teach; it sets out to enlighten. Sacred reading is intent on bringing us face to face with now, of letting us escape nothing in life, of enabling us to bring now to fullness. Like Paul, many of us have been more intent on the things of this world than on the spiritual life. Like Peter, many of us have betrayed the mind of Christ at company board meetings and family picnics. Like Mary, most of us have been asked to do something difficult, impossible, in our daily struggle to bring God's Word to life.

The daily reading of Scripture, *lectio*, is the monastic practice designed to remind us always of who we are and what we have yet to grow into in this particular moment in life if we, too, are to be bearers of the Word. But listening and reading and sharing life with others is not enough. Benedictine spirituality calls us to do as well as to be.

Another tool of the spiritual craft is stewardship. This

monastic practice says that what is good we must work to preserve. In my monastery some of the furniture is almost a hundred years old. "Your antiques are beautiful," people say. And we say, "What antiques?" The fact that things are old does not necessarily render them obsolete. Benedictine spirituality, on the contrary, simply does not believe in indiscriminate consumption. If a thing still works, we keep it and we use it gently so that it will work indefinitely. If it's broken, we repair it, and if it's usable, we develop it, and if it's available, we share it. Stewardship, we believe, is what links the creature to the Creator in a genuine and life-giving way.

Finally, manual labor, too, is commitment to the stewardship of the earth to such a degree that we bear the responsibility for it in our own bodies. No work is beneath the monastic. No work is too small. No effort is too much for those who value the earth and take seriously the responsibility of caring for it.

More than that, manual labor, work with our hands, is work that makes everyone equal. The rich do not sweep faster or better than the poor; the educated do not wash clothes better than the illiterate; the professional does not shovel snow more easily than the farm laborer; the cleric does not change automobile oil with more delicacy than the mechanic. Manual labor is humility in practice.

Benedictine asceticism—fidelity to the commandments of God, the creation of human community, and a commitment to personal maturity—is manifested in a distinctive attitude of life that values silence and custom and *statio* and *lectio* and stewardship and manual labor and the common table. All of them speak of the holiness of life. All of them develop insight in us rather than learning.

All of them plunge us into life rather than take us out of it. All of them require us to look and look again at things until we see them right. Abba Anthony is reported to have said once, "Some have afflicted their bodies by asceticism, but they lack discernment, and so they are far from God." The end of Benedictine asceticism is not spiritual legerdemain. The end of Benedictine asceticism is awareness and wisdom.

The function of Benedictine spirituality, you see, is simply the cultivation of monastic mindfulness.

14

Peace: Sign of the Disarmed Heart

If you desire true and eternal life, "keep your tongue free from vicious talk and your lips from all deceit; turn away from evil and do good; let peace be your quest and aim" (Ps. 33[34]:14–15).

RB PROLOGUE: 17

If you have a dispute with someone, make peace ... before the sun goes down.

RB 4:73

T here is an unfortunate myth about monastic life that has managed to color the spiritual life of both monastics and laity. The idea is that monastic life is free from stress, that there's uninterrupted tranquillity here, that life in a monastery is one long walk with Jesus down a rose-strewn path. As if life in a monastery weren't human. As if life in the monastery weren't its own kind of struggle to grow. As if life in a monastery weren't, as Benedict says in the Rule, the place where "we do battle" to bring the reign of God into our lives and into our worlds (RB Prologue). Over the portals of the great monasteries in Europe, the arch reads, "*Pax*," or peace, true. But what does it mean?

Though I had been waiting for the chance to join a religious community all my young life, it was not easy for me to enter the monastery. I remember the fear and the pain that came with leaving the familiar and the possible behind for the mysterious and the disciplined life of the community. I was, after all, a very young girl and this was a very great, foreboding endeavor, no matter how magnetic it was, no matter how meaningful it was. But then, if it was difficult to enter monastic life, it was often even more difficult to stay. When the great magnetic mystery turned to dailiness and the disciplines turned to frustration, when change shook the Church and community seemed to be disintegrating before our eyes, all the promises of fidelity were tested again and found shaky, sometimes very shaky indeed. Even now, at another stage of my life, the tension is often no less high. Is there nothing we have lived for that we can call achieved: not food for the hungry, not homes for the homeless, not advancement for the underclass, not justice for the people, not peace for the world? Where is the hundredfold, where is the satisfaction, where is the sense of spiritual achievement? What is this Benedictine peace anyway? Is it ever real? And if not here, where? And how?

The answer is plain to see, I have discovered, if you just look carefully at the basic sign of the community. Benedictine women in the United States wear a common ring that was first crafted and worn in the community of Nonnberg, in Salzburg, Austria, in the year 1348. That ring has been worn by every generation since.

It's a very simple ring and it's very Benedictine. The ring itself tells us everything we need to know about Benedictine peace.

The ring design is stark and clear. The letters *IHS*, the

Greek insignia for Jesus that was prescribed by Pilate at the time of the crucifixion to identify the executed Christ, are inscribed on the face of the ring. They are superimposed above three nail heads and are topped by the cross. Palm fronds circle the band of the ring. It is not what you would call an elegant design, but it is indeed a distinctive one. It is, in fact, the sign of what is really given with the legacy of Benedictine peace. The ring, you come to understand as the years go by, is the ring both of the cross and of the palm fronds, both of Good Friday and of Easter Sunday. The ring is the mark of consistent commitment, through good things and bad, through struggle and doubt, through suffering and hope with the sureness of heart that says that the struggle is worth it, that the struggle is blessed, that even the struggle itself is joy.

The message is obvious and after you wear the ring for the greater part of your life, finally the understanding begins to sink in. Real Benedictine peace comes from living the Paschal mystery well, from being willing to die to things that keep us from the fullness of life, from confronting culture with the memory of the cross, from letting nothing deter us from the will of God in life, from living immersed in Christ to such a degree that eventually nothing else matters and witness becomes an imperative.

Benedictine peace comes from being one with creation, from being in harmony with the universe, from rising above ourselves to the peace of Christ, which the world definitely does not give and which confounds the understanding of people who have been led to believe that peace is the absence of conflict or control by force. Benedictine peace comes from trying over and over again to find our place in the universe without violence, without selfishness, without demands.

Benedictine peace is not something that is ever achieved. It is something sincerely and consistently sought. It comes, in fact, from the seeking, not from the getting. It comes from the inside, not the outside. It comes from right-heartedness, not from self-centeredness. It comes from the way we look at life, not from the way we control it. It comes from the attitudes we bring to things, not from the power we bring to them. The Desert Monastics tell a story that draws the distinctions well:

As the army occupied the village, many of the soldiers showed great cruelty in regard to the subjugated people. The most chosen objects of their atrocities were the monastics. So as foreign forces invaded the small towns and hamlets, the monastics fled to the mountains.

When the invaders arrived in one of the villages, however, the leader of the village reported to the commander, "All the monastics, hearing of your approach, fled to the mountains."

And the commander smiled a broad, cold smile, for he was proud of having a reputation for being a very fearsome person.

But then the leader added, "All, that is, but one."

The commander became enraged. He marched to the monastery and kicked in the gate. There in the courtyard stood the one remaining monastic. The commander glowered at the figure. "Do you not know who I am?" the commander demanded. "I am he who can run you through with a sword without batting an eyelash."

And the monastic fixed the commander with a serene and patient look and said, "And do you not know who I am? I am one who can let you run me through with a sword without batting an eyelash."

Monastic peace, in other words, is the power to face what is with the serenity of faith and the courage of hope, with the surety that good can come from evil and the certainty that good will triumph. Peace is the fruit of Benedictine spirituality. Peace is the sign of the disarmed heart .

Benedictine spirituality is a spirituality consciously designed to disarm the heart. Benedict wants monastics to be at peace with what has been given, at peace with what they are asked to do, at peace with those who guide them, at peace with one another, and at peace with themselves. "Let those who need more, ask, and let those who don't, be grateful" (RB 34). "Let them honor the elder and love the younger" (RB 4). "If hard and difficult things are commanded let them, if the situation cannot be changed, do what must be done" (RB 68). "Let them not give way to anger or nurse grudges or even think of being deceitful or fail to be kind, or swear peace but think war in their hearts" (RB 4). Be soft with others and you will have peace in your own heart, the Rule implies. Be simple in your needs and you will have peace in your heart, the Rule directs. Be humble in what you demand of life and you will have peace in your heart, the Rule suggests. Be giving in what you take to life and you will have peace in heart, the Rule counsels. Stop the wars within yourself and you will have peace, the Rule teaches. It is the ability to walk through life lightly—without rancor and greed and jealousy and selfishness—that leads, in other words, to Benedictine peace.

Benedictine spirituality structures life with peace in mind as well. In the Benedictine life, there is to be something of everything and not too much of anything. Life, according to the Benedictine tradition, is to have order and balance and quiet to it. Life is not expected to be perfect; life is simply expected to be dealt with reverently.

People who slam doors know nothing about Benedictine peace. Worse, the very act of slamming doors adds to the tensions of life. People who always talk at the top of their voices have nowhere to go under stress except into even wilder anxiety or into black and silent bitterness. People for whom life is a trail of clothes and books and half-done projects and disordered days drive peace into oblivion.

Peace comes from living a measured life. Peace comes from attending to every part of my world in a sacramental way. My relationships are not what I do when I have time left over from work. My family is not something I pay quiet attention to only when all the other parts of my life—the wash, the cleaning, the yard, the parties, the neighbors, the clubs, the career, and the hobbies—are all finished. Reading is not something I do when life calms down. Prayer is not something I do when I feel like it. They are all channels of hope and growth for me. They must all be given their due. And, Benedictine spirituality implies, they must all be given only their due.

The Rule is very clear about what it takes to live in peace. Peace comes from not needing to control everything and not needing to have everything and not needing to surpass everyone and not needing to know everything and not needing to have everyone else be like me. Peace comes from seeking God in the present and seeing the world as a whole. To treat any single fragment of life as if it were all of life is to turn a single vision of good into a consuming and fanatic disruption of the actual rhythm of life.

Benedictine spirituality with its emphasis on prayer and work and listening and the other, on order and silence and balance, on humility and patience and contemplative consciousness is an invitation to personal peace. It says that life is an excursion into consciousness and quality and calm. It says that only life lived with passion for all its parts can possibly lead us to a sense of harmony.

Peace, our world says, comes from being able to escape stress or reject responsiblity or assure our superiority. Peace, the Rule says, comes from not allowing any part of us to consume the rest of us. When fear of failure haunts us, peace is not possible. When fear of the other erodes our ability to trust, peace is not possible. When life is always lived at high speed, peace is not possible. When what we have means more to us than what we are, peace is not possible. When ambition eats at our hearts and our schedules and our goals and our sense of self, peace is not possible. When consumption is more important to us than contemplation, peace is not possible. When people are more of a bother than a revelation to us, then peace is not possible. When idleness is more our vision of the good life than creative productivity, then peace is not possible. When profit means more to us than quality of life, then peace is not possible. When these things fray our nerves and waste our days and disturb our nights, then our souls have dried and frozen.

The Rule of Benedict has another whole way of living life in mind. Take time for everything, the Rule says. Don't miss the goodness in anything. Remember that life has many dimensions, explore them all. Remember that life does not end here. This life is not our only goal. Life is not something to be hoarded; it is something to be savored and something to be shared. The Rule shows us that peace comes when we end the war within ourselves.

But war within ourselves is always a prelude to war outside ourselves. All war starts within our own hearts.

When our egos are inflated or our desires insatiable, we go to war with the other for the sad joy of maintaining our one-dimensional worlds.

In the face of all of this, the Rule of Benedict offers a model of peace that depends on being gentle with ourselves, gentle with the other, and gentle with the earth. It is a vision of nonviolence that Benedictine spirituality gives a world for which violence is the air it breathes, the songs it sings, the heroes it worships, the business it does.

- Imagine a world where small children are not jerked down supermarket aisles in the name of discipline.
- Imagine a world where it's possible to watch television for one whole night, on any station, and not be subjected to shootouts and beatings and muggings in the name of entertainment.
- Imagine a world where young people are able to find good jobs without having to be part of a war machine designed to destroy the earth in the name of defense.
- Imagine a world where other races and nations and peoples are not demonized to justify our militarism.
- Imagine a world where differences are resolved by force of character rather than by force of arms.
- Imagine a world where the peace of Christ with its prophetic honesty and reckless compassion and nonviolent resistance to evil is the rule of the country.
- But more important perhaps, for now, simply imagine a home where the members of the family do not shout at one another or steal one another's possessions or restrict one another's movements or slap

one another into subjection or bully one another into compliance or intimidate one another into domestic slavery. That would be a Benedictine home.

- Imagine a home where children were taught that those things were wrong, even in the name of patriotism. That would be a Benedictine home.
- Imagine a home where being a little girl did not make a child a less promising being or give her any less to hope for. That would be a Benedictine home.
- Imagine a home where being a little boy did not mean having to prove himself with his fists or his muscles or his willingness to give and take pain. That would be a Benedictine home.
- Imagine a home where both its women and its men could cry. That would be a Benedictine home.
- Imagine a home that taught its children to evaluate the laws and actions of the country according to the laws of God: thou shalt not lie; thou shalt not steal; thou shalt not kill; thou shalt not covet; thou shalt not make false gods. That would be a Benedictine home.
- Equality and reverence and personal differences and the building of community and listening to the Word of God would all be paramount in a place like this. And that would be very Benedictine.
- Imagine a home where all these Benedictine values began to ooze out into the neighborhood and nation around it, and nonviolent resistance became a way of life. Imagine a nation where we would help one another to struggle for truth and justice but never, never with murder in our hearts or blood on our hands.

- Imagine how difficult it would be then to make war or practice segregation or refuse starving refugees. Governments would be forced to come right out and honestly slaughter the unarmed innocent rather than be able to justify their crimes in the name of having to defend themselves against mad and malicious revolutionaries. No one was sure, for instance, that the militant Malcolm X was right in his armed war against a white, racist state, but everyone knew, even in pre-civil rights U.S.A., that to send attack dogs against college boys and preachers at a lunch counter in Atlanta or guns and bombs against girls in a church choir was a sin. Everyone knew that there was something wrong about using fire hoses on peaceful protesters, but everyone knew, too, that for a tired black lady to sit down on a bus at the end of her work day, segregation laws or no segregation laws, was certainly right. Nonviolence is a strong defense. Nonviolence is not passive; nonviolence is simply nondestructive.

The Benedictine worldview says be gentle with yourself, be gentle with the other, be gentle with the earth. Give to others whatever they need (RB 34). Care for the stranger with the best you have (RB 61). Listen to one another (RB 3). Be kind of speech to one another (RB 31). Take care of the guest and the sick and the children and the traveler and everyone in the community whoever they are, rich or poor, young or old, titled or not (RB 30, 38, 53, 55, 59, 63). Handle everything with reverence (RB 32). And work for the good of all (RB 48).

It was to Benedictine monasteries that refugees streamed in the Middle Ages. It was Benedictines who sought to make warfare a moral matter in the Middle Ages. It was Benedictines who demonstrated that all classes of society—cleric and lay, young and old, slave and free, Romans and foreigners—could live together as sisters and brothers in Christ.

Benedictine spirituality intends a nonviolent world where the least favored, the most needy, the totally defenseless are protected and heard and provided for with justice. In the Prophetic Book of Baruch, God names the Chosen "the Peace of Justice." Benedictine spirituality brings this model of peace-through-justice to every place it builds and breaths.

Peace is not monastic romanticism. Peace is a monastic mission. Benedictine peace flows from the scriptural vision of the mandate to co-create the Kingdom, to "till and nurture and tend the Garden" (Gen 2:15) that has been left to us. "The heavens are yours," Psalm 18 reads in the monastic Office, "but the earth you have given to us." Indeed.

And how shall we achieve this peace in our hearts, our homes, and our nation? The symbols of the Paschal mystery—the marks of the cross and the palm fronds and nails—on the monastic ring give the answer. We cannot expect life to be without struggle, perhaps. We cannot expect life to be perfect. But we can expect to see life come from death. We can expect to see morning after night. We can expect that acceptance of the struggle will give rise to the victory over self. We can expect that commitment to struggle against the forces of chaos within us and around us will bring the energy that love always brings. We can expect that dying for the other will bring us to new life within ourselves. We can expect the enemy to see the face of God where there is no violent response.

And to support this mystery there is a growing body of data. Historians point to the effectiveness of nonviolent resistance against the Germans in France and the English in India and the segregationists in the United States. Psychologists are beginning to warn us that anger unrestrained in the interests of "expressing our emotions" simply generates more anger. Communication theorists point out again and again that people most commonly respond in the key in which they've been addressed. And social psychologists document clearly the effect of violence on the emotional, social, and intellectual development of abused children and battered wives and beaten dogs.

Violence is getting us nowhere. Benedictine spirituality calls us beyond all of that by demanding personal dignity and mutual respect and listening. Order and quiet and regularity and Scripture and work, all done in the interest of the coming of the Kingdom in our hearts and in our world, keep us from becoming frenetic, from becoming narcissistic, from becoming demanding, from becoming our own gods. Peace comes when we realize our place in the universe and refuse to inflate it.

But do not be misled. Peace is not passivity. It takes great effort and continual commitment and the humdrum of years of dailiness to make the world come down right, to come down loving and equal in the home and the world. It means that every day we have to learn to curb our own urge for power and to resist the propaganda designed to make enemies of strangers.

Peace is a by-product of humility. And humility is always honest; it is just never arrogant, never pushy, never destructive. No, humility convicts simply by its accusing presence and courageous evaluations of what is patently wrong but never open to discussion: the arms race, slavery, wife beating, the national debt, human poverty in a nation of plenty.

The peace you see in the life of Christ clamors for justice so that others, like us, may take their own right places in the universe as well. Benedictine peace calls us to value that other. Benedictine peace is founded on justice: give to the poor; be open to the stranger; care for the weak; respect one another; be gentle with one another; work for the community; guard the earth. The Rule requires it.

Then comes the serenity of the one who can be run through with the sword without batting an eye. Then comes the fullness of the mystery of the ring.

15

The Monastic Vision: Gift for a Needy World

[N]ow that we have asked God who will dwell in the holy tent, we have heard the instruction for dwelling in it, but only if we fulfill the obligations of those who live there. We must, then, prepare our hearts and bodies for the battle of holy obedience to his instructions. What is not possible to us by nature, let us ask the Holy One to supply by the help of grace. If we wish to reach eternal life, then—while there is still time, while we are in this body and have time to accomplish all these things by the light of life—we must run and do now what will profit us forever.

RB PROLOGUE:39–44

The chapel in our monastery is one entire wing of the house. It has a soaring cathedral ceiling that rises majestically from a sloping floor. The east and west walls that frame the space are stained-glass from the ceiling almost to the baseboards. The altar stands starkly in the center of the sanctuary. Live plants grow profusely at its edges as if nourished from this spring of living water.

It's a beautiful chapel and a fairly traditional one, except for one thing. The chapel doors are glass. All glass. People have been known to walk into them, in fact, unaware of their presence. From the altar, then, the foyer is a clear view. From the foyer, the altar makes a magnetic center. Each is to the other a necessity. To be at the altar is to be drawn away from it. To be in the foyer is to be drawn toward it. I have a notion that that is about all there is to say about Benedictine spirituality.

There's an ancient story that explains the gift of Benedictine life to the modern world.

Once upon a time, the story begins, some seekers from the city asked the local monastic a question:

"How does one seek union with God?"

And the Wise One said, "The harder you seek, the more distance you create between God and you."

"So what does one do about the distance?" the seekers asked.

And the elder said simply, "Just understand that it isn't there."

"Does that mean that God and I are one?" the disciples said.

And the monastic said, "Not one. Not two."

"But how is that possible?" the seekers insisted.

And the monastic answered, "Just like the sun and its light, the ocean and the wave, the singer and the song. Not one. But not two."

When Benedict of Nursia wrote his ancient Rule in the sixth century, he did not write a manual of spiritual exercises or a codex of canon laws. The Rule was not an excursion into the occult or the mystical or even the grimly ascetic. The Rule of Benedict was a document designed simply to make people conscious of the God-life in which they are already immersed. The Rule of Benedict set out to make the normal and the natural the stepping stones of the Holy. The Rule of Benedict was written by a lay prophet in the church who understood humanity and lived it without apology.

Benedictine spirituality, then, rests on elements that have meaning in our own time: prayer, *lectio* (reflective reading of Scripture), community, balance, humility, mindfulness, obedient listening, and stewardship of the earth. Never before in history have those elements been needed more.

Benedict teaches us to this day that prayer is more than the recitation of prayers of petition. Prayer is the putting on of the mind of Christ so that we learn to see the world as God sees it. Benedictine prayer is not designed to change God or to coax God to save me from my selfish self. No, prayer in the Rule of Benedict is designed to change me, to open me to the in-breaking of the Spirit in life today, to stretch me beyond my own agendas to take on the compassionate heart of Christ. Prayer in Benedictine spirituality is not an exercise or a discipline. Prayer is the act of recognizing that life is infused with the Divine and that, whatever I am, I am capable of being more. Prayer, in Benedictine spirituality, is not only for consolation and courage, it is for challenge as well.

Lectio, or the reflective reading of Scripture that Benedict mandates for the serious Christian, is meant to make me see that the Scriptures were written for me, to me, that my own life is an Exodus story, a salvation story, a crucifixion story, a resurrection story and that, as the cycles of my life change, I become a different character in each of the scenarios. I have known what it is to be Nathan and not use my influence to save the poor who depend on me. I have known what it is to be Samuel, to be called and called and called and not recognize the Voice. I have known what it is to be Mary and to be rejected for doing what the will of God demands of me now.

In *lectio*, I come to new understandings of my own life. Sometimes, like Nicodemus, I have preferred to approach Jesus at night rather than to speak his beatitudes in the full light of the office or the party or the club. But, in *lectio*, too, I discover that Nicodemus finally is able to break with social expectations, spend himself to claim Jesus' body, care for it, and pay the cost of doing that. *Lectio*, in other words, gives us depth of understanding and energy and promise.

For Benedict of Nursia, community was the place in which we worked out our own responsibility to continue the task of creating a just and gentle world. Benedictine spirituality calls us to bear with one another and hold one another up and call one another to growth and so become whole and holy ourselves. It's in the community of my neighborhood and family that I learn my own weaknesses and can give all my gifts. It is in community that I discover the effect of a spoiled ozone layer on everyone else and can work to save them as well as myself. It is in community that I see the evils of sexism with its unnatural limitations on both women and men and can bend myself to making the book of Genesis complete. It is in community that I see the lie of national chauvinism and can work to make my own nation more kind. It is in the community of my own life that I can begin to build a better life.

To a nonstop world, the Rule of Benedict brings balance and simplicity. In the face of a complex world with its twenty-four-hour workdays and constant motion, the Rule asks for a life that deals with a little bit of everything in proper measure: work, prayer, solitude, relationships. The Rule, in other words, is an antidote to excess and to human dwarfism. A proverb says, "Wherever there is excess, something is lacking." The Rule of Benedict mandates a measured life.

The Rule of Benedict says to our times, too, that humility is more important than power, that arrogance is destructive of the human spirit and, in our case perhaps, of the world itself. Humility is the quality that calls us to let God be God in our personal lives and to take our proper place among all the creatures of the earth. Humility says that to hold the world hostage to nuclear weapons when we need food and housing and medical care and negotiation, is arrogance raised to high art. Humility says that we must all learn to listen and to hear, to negotiate rather than to force, to trust rather than to terrorize, in both our neighborhoods and our nations.

Monastic mindfulness is what concentrates us on the right things in life. When we learn to be aware of what is around us as well as in us, we begin to connect with the rest of the world in new ways. We become conscious of little things and their beauty. We come to see obscure things and their meaning. We are touched by quiet things and their power.

When we learn to be where we are, we gain perspective on life. Yesterday loses its hold on us and tomorrow loses it allure. Where we are becomes the ground of our salvation, the reason for our joy and the acme of our achievement. Monastic mindfulness calms the storms of life and gives them meaning. Monastic mindfulness makes the present, present and gives us back the energy that endless worry and constant calculation drain. It concentrates what has become scattered and brings us home to ourselves.

Obedient listening teaches us critical discernment. When we are overcome by all the cacophonous com-

mercials and unrelenting demands and spurious advice
that our society has to give, obedient listening is what
enables us to filter all the messages through channels that
count: the good, the true, and the beautiful. Obedient listening evaluates everything, not in the light of what is
good for me but in the light of what is best for all of us.
It is the call to bring the foolish standards of the gospel
to the issues of our times. Obedient listening is designed
to bring us to growth, to truth, and to holy responsibility—for our own lives and for the lives of the entire human community.

The call to "treat all things as if they were the vessels
of the altar" (RB 31:10) is the call to steward the earth,
to treat it reverently, to hold it in loving hands. It is the
call to keep what is usable, to care for what is vulnerable,
to safeguard what is fragile on this planet. It is the call to
preserve the environment and to clean our houses and
our streets and our woods and to stop pollution. It is the
call to save the earth for our children.

The twenty-first century is indeed a Benedictine century. We need stability in relationships, creation rather
than destruction in the works we do, a Christian attitude
toward life and a commitment to balance that slows the
frenetic pace of our personal lives, our family lives, and
our national lives. Benedictine spirituality offers all of that
and more.

The Rule of Benedict was a spiritual document written
for males raised in Imperial Rome. But to Roman men in
a patriarchal culture who were trained that domination
and status and power were their birthright and their purpose in life, the Rule insisted on new ideals: humility,
listening, community, equality, and service. It was a very
feminine vision. It is a vision still very much needed today.

It is family, not social life, that is needed in our time too. It is equality, not domination, that has something to say about the coming of the Kingdom. It is listening, not demanding, that is at the heart of human obedience in a world not controlled by all whites, all males, all Westerners anymore. It is creation, not production and profit, that is at the heart of the gospel.

Benedictine spirituality, then, is first and foremost a practical way to live the good news of the gospel today.

This society is a complex, consumer society; we can be simple. We can reverence creation. We can refuse to have one thing more than we need. We can refuse to hoard one thing we can give away. We can refuse to keep anything we are not using. We can give one thing away for every one thing we receive.

This society is very ambitious and frantic for its own ends. We can be stable. We can use our own lives to indicate that some things—our relationships to one another, the search for God, the meaning of life—never change.

This society exploits. It breaks the backs of sugar workers; it destroys farm workers; it wipes out the working person; it discards the middle-aged and forgets the elderly. We can minister to the world by calling for justice.

This society dominates and is selfish and has its own goals as the inner force of its life. We can be community. We can say by our lives that there are times when it is important for us to step back in life so that others can gain.

This society depends on power. We can practice the power of the powerless who show us all how little it really takes to live, how rich life is without riches, how strong are those who cannot be owned, how clear is the gospel about the rights of the poor. We can be the voice of those who are not heard and the hands of those who have no bread and the families of those who are alone and the strength of those who are weak. We can be the sign of human community.

Finally, this society is anxious and angry and noisy. We can be contemplative. In the midst of chaos, if the Scripture is in our hearts, if we are faithful to *lectio*, if we build the Jesus-life in our own souls, we can see God where God is. Everywhere.

Those are the new asceticisms and those are the new graces and those are the new revelations of God in our day. Those, then, must become the way we express faith in our times. Those are the dust and breath of the new spirituality. Those are the elements of Benedictine vision that saved the Western world over the centuries again and again and again. And they can save us from ourselves once more. Benedictine spirituality does not call for spiritual athletes; Benedictine spirituality calls for spiritual giants who know that God is in our dailiness, calling us and converting us to a vision far beyond our own.

It is the ancients who may best explain the process and the substance of Benedictine spirituality:

"Where shall I look for Enlightenment?" the disciple asked.
"Here," the elder said.
"When will it happen?" the disciple wanted to know.
"It is happening right now," the elder said.
"Then why don't I experience it?" the disciple asked.
And the elder answered, "Because you do not look."
"But what should I look for?" the disciple wanted to know.
And the elder smiled and answered, "Nothing. Just look."
"But at what?" the disciple insisted.
"Anything your eyes alight upon," the elder continued.
"Well, then, must I look in a special kind of way?" the disciple said.

"No," the elder said.

"Why ever not?" the disciple persisted.

And the elder said quietly, "Because to look you must be here. The problem is that you are mostly somewhere else."

In each of those insights may lie the spirit of Benedictine spirituality.

Spirituality has seldom been a major topic in the average theology curriculum or even the greatest concern of the ecclesiastical community. What the classics said prayer was, prayer was. What the formulas said was how God was to be found, was how God was to be found. For everybody. At all times. And especially for the laity who were clearly to be the consumers, not the providers, of religion or spiritual exercises or spiritual direction. But the Rule of Benedict requires that we set down and describe for ourselves in what ways God is most real and present in our lives, with or without formulas, with or without the standard images and exercises.

The ascetic, the mystical, even the liturgical streams of spirituality all seem to presuppose the building of sacred bridges from here to there. But Benedictine spirituality says that God is in the fabric of our worn lives: not in incense and purple so much, it seems, as in people and places that make the Word of God alive by touching our worlds in immediate ways. God acts through others, a communal spirituality declares. God acts in the now. God is here.

There is a great deal of emphasis in Benedictine spirituality on taking time for God and on preparing the mind and heart for the presence of God. But there is equal emphasis on the consciousness that God happens when God happens, and that that is not necessarily on schedule.

For people whose lives are overfull of others and too often devoid of time for self, even in prayer, the disciple's question, "When will it happen?" is often the question that leads beyond despair to emptiness. But no one ever took much time to lift that guilt or mend that feeling of brokenness in the soul. God was something that happened to cloistered contemplatives, or to monastics in general, or at least to religious, or surely to priests. The worker-bee types—the laity, the mothers, the fathers with two jobs, the secretaries—went to church on Sunday, did their Easter duty, said their novenas, and waited for heaven. In the meantime, God consorted intimately with different types. But Benedictine spirituality calls everyone to see the sanctity of who they are and what they do, the porter as well as the priest in the community, the table server as well as the prioress, the last in rank as well as the abbot.

The nineteenth century spiritual writer de Caussade talked a great deal about the sacrament of the present moment, and certainly the psalmists walked with God through the dailiness of life. For the most part, though, contemplation was considered a great deal more difficult than that: something to be studied and exercised. But then you read the Rule of Benedict with its attention to humility and listening and simple stewardship as the cornerstones of sanctity and you get the distinct impression, with the ancient elder, that what has been the popular currency of the spiritual life may also, indeed, have been counterfeit.

When God has become a business, though, it is very hard for people to get the confidence to realize that God is really a personal God, a God who touches us as individuals, a God who is as close to us as we choose to see. We have learned well the remoteness of a God who lived for so long behind communion rails and altar steps and seminary doors and chancery desks that the experience of God, however strong, has always been more private secret than public expectation.

For most people, the talents they have must be pointed out by others for them to realize there is something in themselves worth developing. The spiritual life is hardly any different. How do we know if we even have a spirituality if no one ever asks and no one ever invites us to lend our secrets? Like the musician who never learned to play, or the artist who never took drawing lessons, or the writer who has never been read, a person whose spiritual life goes unrecognized never learns to trust the gift themselves. Benedictine spirituality calls us to share our spiritual lives together, to nurture them together, and to learn from one another. When someone is having a hard time understanding the ways of God in life, the Rule says, send a wise and prudent person to help them work the thing through (RB 27:2–3). Reveal all the thoughts of your heart to the abbot, the Rule instructs, so that what is unworthy can be dashed against the Rock that is Christ before it grows up to scar the spirit (RB 4:50).

There is nothing easier in spirituality than to lead people down the path of prayer forms without ever asking them what goes on inside of them as a result. At the end, consequently, it is possible to get a praying person; it is not always possible to get a spiritual person. Praying people get their prayers in and wait for God somehow miraculously to deliver them from their private demons. Spiritual people expect the demons. What they look for is a way to find God even there. The Rule of Benedict tells us to accept our personal weaknesses, to see them as the road to humility and community, to stay the course no matter the tide.

"Learn to see what you're looking at and then say what you see," a wise old professor told me once. That advice, the elder seems to indicate, holds for the spiritual life as well. Learning to look at our worlds as if they were really made by God, as if God were really in them now, as if God were calling to us from the other side of every event and situation is different from rushing about trying to find God somewhere else. But learning to look is so difficult in a culture that is highly technological and intent on fixing what is not broken. Nothing is ever good enough here. What might be is always so much more important to us than what is. And so the Presence becomes a distant possibility rather than a personal reality. But Benedictine spirituality says that the Now is holy and full of God and to be savored and suffused with the consciousness of the God of time.

And what are we to concentrate on to find God? Are we to look at the God of the theology books? Are we to look at the God held in bondage by the males of the Church? Are we to concentrate on the God of the syllogisms and the schools of philosophy? Are we to look only at the male father figure who has no woman in him? Or is there someplace deep in ourselves where a God of greater dimensions, with all gender and with no gender at all, seeps out to cloak the entire world in life and goodness? Benedictine spirituality says that to find God we must all find the feminine parts of ourselves in obedient listening and a community of relationships and the power of humility. Benedictine spirituality says that God is where I am. More than that, it implies, God is where you are. But those are hard words for the rationalists, for the secularists, for the chauvinists, for those with no self, no self-worth, no self-esteem, no self-identity.

Indeed, the how-does-one-become-holy question is as old as the Exodus and the answers are just as varied: keep the laws; go up the mountain; walk with God; do not worship idols, follow the cloud by day and the fire by night. But not everybody did all those things. And not everyone did any of them the same way. They were a motley—but a chosen—people. For centuries we have been following the lights of others. The Rule of Benedict says that we must learn to follow our own call, our own lives, to find what is sanctifying for us.

Real spiritual wisdom knows that God is unique to every unique being. Real spiritual wisdom knows that spirituality is not packaged and not processed and not produced for the mass market. Real spirituality is something that brings us now in touch with God here. It does not take formulas or *imprimaturs*. It takes consciousness.

The easy way out, of course, is to take the package deal. To let religious formulas substitute for spirituality. To allow others to digest our God for us. The valiant thing, the committed thing, the graced thing, is to believe that we ourselves are good enough to contain God for ourselves. But we have all been taught differently from that. We have all been taught, whoever we are, that God is just a notch beyond and above and unlike ourselves. It is time to find out where God really is for us.

Once upon a time, the story goes, a preacher ran through the streets of the city shouting, "We must put God into our lives. We must put God into our lives." And hearing him, an old monastic rose up in the city plaza to say, "No, sir, you are wrong. You see, God is already in our lives. Our task is simply to recognize that."

It is to the recognition of God in our own lives that the Rule of Benedict calls us.

Appendix: Benedictinism, Its Foundation and Rule

Benedictinism is the most influential form of cenobitic religious life in the Western world. Men and women who devoted themselves to the spiritual life before the time of Benedict of Nursia in 480 C.E. did so largely as hermits or as disciples gathered around a spiritual guide. Benedict, though, drew disciples together into stable groups whose spirituality depended as much on their relationship to one another as it did on their deference to their abbot. The effect was to create a sense of the social as well as the private dimension of the spiritual life.

The Rule of Benedict is one of the oldest living documents in the Western world. It was written in sixth-century Italy and has been used as a spiritual guide in the Western world for nearly fifteen hundred years. Thousands of women and men around the world live by it still. More than that, thousands of lay people, Benedictine Oblates and Associates, Roman Catholic and Anglican, in every country are even today attempting to refocus their own lives and private worlds around the values of this ancient Rule.

The problem is that unless people stumble on to it through associations with Benedictines themselves, the

Rule is hardly accessible to the public except through academic or historical studies. The text itself, though short—less than a hundred small pages in any format—and simple to read, is also obscured by its language and development. Very few people, for instance, can read chapter seven of the Rule of Benedict, "On Humility," in this day and age and make sense out of it. This book is an attempt to make the Rule accessible to the laity of our own times.

To do that, it is important to understand a little of the history and the structure of the Rule.

Benedict of Nursia was born in Italy in ca. 480. He went to school in Rome when the Empire was in a state of material prosperity but moral decline. In the midst of all of that, he decided that life lived in that fashion was not the fullness of life at all. He left Rome and went to a rural area south of the city to contemplate the meaning of life, to simplify its demands, and to refashion his own attitudes and life-style.

It wasn't long until he was sought after by multitudes of other people who were also uneasy with the secular climate of the day but unsure as well of what ought to be its spiritual character. Out of this came what we know today as Western monasticism, the pursuit of the spiritual life in community, rather than in the secluded cells of the solitaries, which was the form of religious life that had been prevalent in the deserts of Egypt and in the East. Under the influence of Pope Gregory the Great, the Benedictine Rule began to be widely diffused in Europe. The Rule was embraced due to its moderation, its popularity among average people, and its endorsement by rulers who saw the values of work and stability essential to the development of the area. As time passed, Benedictine monasteries became the anchor points and centerpieces of whole villages in Europe. From the monastics of the place the people learned to live and to work and to pray. As a result, the Benedictine Order has often been credited with having saved Western Europe after the barbarian invasions, and Benedict himself was named the patron of Europe. To Benedict and to the monastics who followed him, in other words, spirituality had a highly social dimension.

As a result, the Rule that arose out of life lived in common consists of seventy-two chapters on how to live with others, how to deal with life's normal demands, and how to develop a spiritual life capable of living in the real world and being attentive to the Spirit at the same time.

The Rule is best understood when it's seen in four parts: Part One, chapters 1–7, the spiritual document, sets out the basic values of Benedictine life; Part Two, chapters 8–20, structures the prayer life of the community; Part Three, chapters 21–70, demonstrates how the values of the Rule are to be applied in the daily life and structure of the monastery; and Part Four, chapters 71–72, reflect on the place of a Rule in life and the nature of good zeal, or real spirituality, in a sea of counterfeits.

From its earliest beginnings, the Rule was lived both by monastics in their monasteries and by consecrated virgins in their homes. It became in fact the spiritual model and leader of whole areas, much as parish models and diocesan directives have been in our own time. From France in the sixth century to Ireland to England and then, under the patronage of Charlemagne, to the continent as a whole, the Benedictine Rule of life had by the eighth century slowly and steadily replaced all other monastic documents of the time as the Rule of choice in monasteries throughout Europe. By the eleventh century a great outpouring of Benedictine life among both men and women, nobles and commoners, elite and uneducated— black Benedictines and Cistercians,—gave witness to the vitality of the Rule and its widespread spiritual appeal.

A plethora of social changes—the rise of nation-states, urbanization, democratization, and massive emigration patterns—led to the rise of multiple other forms of religious life. At the same time, the Black Death and the Hundred Years War resulted in the loss of vitality and, in some cases, even the extinction of some Benedictine houses. Almost half of the monasteries disappeared in the sixteenth century due to the repressive measures of the Reformation. In England, for instance, Benedictine monasteries were totally suppressed and later, in France, the Revolution closed the monasteries en masse. But by the nineteenth century, a Benedictine revival led by Dom Prosper Gueranger in the monastery at Solesmes, France, began a new period in Benedictine history. Most of the monasteries existing today can trace their own beginnings to this nineteenth century renewal of Benedictine life.

At this same time, a reemphasis on the missionary spirit of Benedictinism coupled with the increasing numbers of German emigrants to the New World led to the implantation of Benedictine monasticism from Germany to the United States. Abbot Boniface Wimmer of Metten Abbey in Bavaria and Prioress Benedicta Riepp of St. Walburga Abbey in Eichstätt, Bavaria, began the first foundations of Benedictine monks and nuns in the United States in Pennsylvania in the 1850s.

Now, according to the 1985 *Catalogus* of the Benedictine Order published by the Benedictine Confederation in Rome, there are 373 communities of Benedictine men with 9,453 monks and 478 communities of Benedictine women with 19,989 nuns and sisters in the world today. Of those, 50 communities of Benedictine women with 5,123 sisters and 47 communities of Benedictine men with 2,316 monks are in the United States. Each of them follows the Rule of Benedict to this day.

In addition to these individual communities, many of the monasteries sponsor groups of lay Oblates and Associates who are formally committed to the individual monastery in question and who apply the Rule of Benedict to the married or single state of life.

Glossary

ABBESS. The elected leader of a Benedictine community of nuns.

ABBOT. The elected leader of a Benedictine community of monks.

ACEDIA. A lethargy that makes the continued efforts of the spiritual life too much for the soul.

BASIL. Bishop of Caesarea and a Doctor of the Church, that is, a major teacher, he was born in Asia Minor about 329 CE. He preached a communal use of property, charity as an incentive to labor, and opposed the disparity among social classes.

BENEDICTINE ASSOCIATE. A lay person who interacts with the Benedictine community in prayer, community life and ministry.

BENEDICTINE OBLATE. A lay person who shares the spiritual life of the monastic community.

BREVIARY. A book which contains the seasonal parts of the liturgy of the hours, the breviary appeared as the Divine Office became fixed in form and content.

CASSIAN. A fifth century monk and spiritual writer whose works contain historically important descriptions of monasticism and statements of the problems of the spiritual life.

CENOBITE. A member of a religious community whose chief ministry is community itself. Cenobitic communities differ from apostolic institutes in that, for cenobites, their apostolic ministries flow from their community lives.

CENOBITIC. Adjective describing those who live in a monastic community under a rule and an abbot.

CENSER. A vessel in which incense is burned.

CHAPTER. The deliberative body of a monastic community. It is made up of the perpetually professed members of the community and is called and led by the abbot, the abbess, or the prioress.

CISTERCIANS. A monastic order founded at Citeaux in France in 1098 to live a life of poverty, simplicity and solitude under the Rule of Benedict as strictly interpreted. The Trappists are an offshoot of the Cistercians who dedicated themselves to living a contemplative life when the Cistercians became pastors and teachers.

COMMUNITIES, CLOISTERED. When a community is cloistered, a part of their house and grounds, the enclosure, is reserved to their exclusive use. Such a community rarely leaves their own house and grounds.

COMMUNITY CUSTOMS, BOOK OF. A collection of the specific practices of a particular community.

CONVERSION CONVERSATIO MORUM, Vow of. The vow by which Benedictines commit themselves to follow the monastic way of life, its attitudes and values and practices, in order to come to spiritual fulfillment and development.

DESERT MONASTICS. Men and women who went into the desert and lived deeply ascetic lives devoted to prayer and manual work, often under the direction of a spiritual master. Many of their sayings and stories have been preserved.

DIVINE OFFICE. The traditional term for the Liturgy of the Hours, the choral prayer of a Benedictine monastic community that is comprised of psalms and readings from Scripture. Morning praise and evening praise are the basic hours of the Divine Office though monastic communities commonly pray one or more of the other five traditional hours as well. These are prime, terce, sext, none, and matins.

EASTER VIGIL. The liturgical celebration, on the night before Easter, of the Resurrection of Jesus. Vigil in this context refers, not to the day before Easter, but to the fact that the liturgy is held at night, as is the more familiar vigil, Midnight Mass on Christmas.

EREMITICAL LIFE. Religious life distinguished by solitude and austerity.

EREMITICAL TRADITION. The manifestation of solitary life more than two thousand years old. By the fourth century, church authorities began to regulate hermits' lives, requiring them to live near a monastery under the supervision of the abbot. The Carthusians and Camaldolese maintain this form of the eremitic life today.

FEAST DAYS. Days of religious celebration, usually annual, which honor a saint or memorialize an event.

FORMATION PROGRAM. Several years of study and experience intended to teach the fundamentals of Benedictinism and monastic practice to those preparing for perpetual profession.

GLORY BE. The first words and, by extension, the title of a short prayer in honor of the Trinity; i.e., Glory be the Father, and to the Son, and to the Holy Spirit.

HOLY DAY. A holiday or feast day on which attendance at a particular religious observance is obligatory.

HOLY WATER. Water blessed for use in religious observance.

HORARIUM. The daily schedule of activities.

JANSENISM. A seventeenth century European heresy which saw human nature as corrupt, to be kept under control by rigorous penance and rigid insistence on the pursuit of perfection.

LECTIO. The meditative reading of the Scriptures in order to gain inspiration and understanding of the Christian life through the filter of the Word of God.

LITURGY OF THE HOURS. Current term for *Opus Dei*, or Divine Office, the choral prayer common to monastic life.

MAGNIFICAT. The hymn of Mary, recorded in Luke 1:46–55, named by its first word in the Latin version.

MONKS. Benedictine men who are either engaged in public ministries or who live a cloistered life, according to the historical nature of the community and the decision of the monastic chapter itself.

MONASTICS. Men or women who live together in community and follow a monastic way Rule of life.

NOVENA. A nine day series of prayers.

NOVICE. A beginner, a neophyte. A monastic novice lives with the community and must fulfill certain canonical regulations prior to full incorporation into the community.

NOVICE MISTRESS. A sister who directs the novices in their preparation for the monastic life. The term "novice director" is commonly used today.

NOVITIATE. Novices collectively, or that part of the house used primarily by the novices.

NOVITIATE TABLE. That table in the dining room where the novices sit. Today, the novices are not usually confined to a specific table.

NUNS. Benedictine women who live a cloistered life.

OBEDIENCE, VOW OF. The vow by which a monastic promises to follow the Rule, the leader of the monastery, and the community in the faithful living of the monastic life.

OPUS DEI. The Latin words used by Benedict in his Rule to describe the choral prayer of the Benedictine community as "The Work of God."

PASCHAL MYSTERY. Refers to the events of Christ's death and resurrection and to the consequent redemption of humanity.

PERPETUAL PROFESSION. The formal act of pronouncing religious vows not limited as to time.

PRIME. See Divine Office.

PRIOR. An official of a house of monks appointed by the abbot or elected by the community, who exercises a determined degree of authority.

PRIORESS. The elected leader of a Benedictine community of sisters.

PRIVATE DEVOTIONS. The individual devotions of a single person, rather than the liturgy of the community together.

RELIGIOUS LIFE. The following of Christ in a way characterized by public commitment to a group, service to the people of God and approval by the Church.

SCAPULAR. That part of the traditional Benedictine habit which, worn over the shoulders, hung to the floor in a straight strip in front and back. It developed from the work apron, later becoming a part of the full habit.

SCHOLASTIC DIRECTOR. One who oversees the formation of scholastics. A scholastic is a Benedictine who has completed the novitiate and has professed vows for a specific period of time as part of the preparation for final, or perpetual, profession.

SCHOLASTICA. Benedict's twin sister, the first Benedictine nun.

SEXT. See Divine Office.

SISTERS. Benedictine women who participate in public ministries.

STABILITY, VOW OF. The vow that binds a monastic to the community life of a particular monastery.

STATIO. The practice of gathering in silence outside of the monastic chapel in order to achieve a spirit of recollection before the community enters the body of the church for choral prayer.

TALMUD. The ancient collection of rabbinic writings which is, for Judaism, the repository of religious authority second only to Sacred Scripture.

TRAPPISTS. See Cistercians.

VIGIL LIGHTS. The small candles left burning in churches and shrines as signs of the prayer of the faithful.